Walking Through Holy Week

A Journey Into the Story of Easter

Karen May

© 2017 by Karen May

All rights reserved.

Excerpts from the *Lectionary for Mass for Use in the Dioceses of the United States of America, second typical edition* © 2001, 1998, 1997, 1986, 1970 Confraternity of Christian Doctrine, Inc., Washington, DC. Used with permission. All rights reserved. No portion of this text may be reproduced by any means without permission in writing from the copyright owner.

Cover and interior design: Kathie Alexander

Published by Karen's Grace, LLC.

ISBN 978-0-9994414-04

For more by Karen May
read her six-week study

Be Not Afraid:
Living with Faith in the Midst of a Fearful World

or find her at www.AmayzingGraces.com

Contents

FORWARD 6
AN INVITATION 8

1. **PALM SUNDAY:** 10
   Triumphal Entry to Tragic Ending

2. **HOLY THURSDAY:** 38
   The Passover Transformed

3. **GOOD FRIDAY PART 1:** 60
   Walking the Road to the Cross

4. **GOOD FRIDAY PART 2:** 92
   The Freely Given Sacrifice

5. **HOLY SATURDAY:** 116
   Waiting Remembering, Rejoicing

6. **EASTER SUNDAY:** 168
   Discovery of a New World

   APPENDIX A 182
   Year B and C Readings

   APPENDIX B 203
   Scripture References

   APPENDIX C 209
   Contradictions in the Passion of Jesus

   APPENDIX D 212
   Parallels to Jesus in the Story of the Sacrifice of Isaac

   NOTES FOR HOLY WEEK 214

Dedication

To Paul Juarez,

for his dedication to all that is meaningful in each and every Mass, and for answering my myriad of questions with patience and joy.

Acknowledgements

I would not be here without my amazing Tuesday writing group. Sara and Simone, I thought that it was all for you, yet look what has happened since. Gillian and Crystal, I've been so blessed by your joining us. But especially, I want to thank Sara. You share your home, you encourage us, and you give us a space that invites us to come and to stay, physically and spiritually. We are greatly blessed.

I can never give thanks enough for my first and favorite editors, Mike, Ashley, and Lindsey. I value your feedback and support more than anything. I love you so much.

And finally, to my faith community at St. John Neumann Catholic Church. You inspire me, challenge me, comfort me, and give me a place to flourish in my faith. Through you, I am often given a very direct look into the heart of Jesus.

Forward

Alice was a good Catholic. She attended Mass every week, took her children to Religious Education, and even started to teach in the classes. The only problem was that she wasn't actually Catholic. She was coming to Mass to support her husband and give her family a consistent faith tradition. She was sending her children to Religious Education to support and develop their faith. It wasn't until she started teaching their classes that she began to feel that her level of participation wasn't enough. She had always felt like an outsider, like she was missing some secret lessons that only the true Catholics understood. As she taught, she started to see that the things that had seemed so foreign and different were actually beautiful and inviting. She wanted more, so she started to attend RCIA[1] classes to formally enter the Catholic Church.

As her Confirmation sponsor and friend, I knew that her understanding of what was happening at Mass was limited. Not only that, but she had never been to the Masses of Holy Week where she would declare her faith and be accepted into the Catholic Church. We sat together in the church a couple of weeks before Easter, and I explained the stories that would be told and the activities that would be in the services of each day. As she stood in front of the congregation that Holy Saturday, waiting to be confirmed with tears streaming down her face, I knew that this week had been powerful for her. I saw that the stories and events of the week were more than just stories being told. As a result, her Confirmation was filled with joy, desire, and love for Jesus and what He had done for her. I have seen that joy and love each week since, and her desire to encounter Jesus in the Mass has never been the same.

---

[1] RITE OF CHRISTIAN INITIATION FOR ADULTS – A FORMATION PROGRAM FOR PEOPLE WANTING TO CONVERT TO THE CATHOLIC FAITH.

I have taught about these Masses for years. I have told these stories to children and adults, and each time, they have transformed the experience of Easter and Holy Week for them.

I have taught about these Masses for years. I have told these stories to children and adults, and each time, they have transformed the experience of Easter and Holy Week for them. Each time, the people who hear them transform from observers in the Mass into active participants. Now it is time that I write it all down, and I offer it to you.

In this study, I hope that you discover the stories that are being told in each Mass, and that you are drawn into them. I pray that you experience the amazement, struggle, joy, sadness, and wonder that are so very real in each day of Holy week. I ask Jesus to allow you to walk by His side as He moves so quickly from His triumphal entry into Jerusalem to complete betrayal and abandonment on the cross, and finally to the glorious victory of the resurrection.

These are the stories of Jesus. These are the stories of his followers. And they are the stories of our lives. God bless you as you surround yourself with them.

An Invitation

Imagine with me for a moment. Pope Francis has been captured by ISIS and has been placed on trial. The scene is being played out in a public forum in front of crowds demanding his execution. He stands in front of the people, having been beaten and tortured, a shadow of the man we know. The evidence has been weak, or completely lacking, and yet the judge hands down a sentence of death. The cost of his heresy will be his life. In ISIS form, the public trial does not end there. The Pope, weakened and bloody, is taken to the countryside, and beheaded on camera for all the world to see.

If you can imagine such a scene, imagine the response that this would spark around the world. Governments would condemn the sham of a trial and the brutal injustice of the sentence. People, regardless of their religious affiliation, would be shocked and outraged at such brazen behavior. We would look on in horror as the events unfolded – confused, saddened, and angered at the senselessness and inhumanity of it all.

These events are real. They are historical. They are shocking and devastating. They are surprising and exhilarating.

In reality, we see something similar every year, and we hardly react at all. Every year on Palm Sunday, we sit calmly making crosses with our palms and listen as Jesus is arrested in the night, presented to Pilate with weak accusations, and placed on trial in front of murderous crowds. We stand, restlessly impatient, as Jesus walks the hill to Calgary, sentenced to a horrific death on a cross. We read along as He is placed in the tomb, and the crowds walk away, the tragedy over and complete. We return home to our busy lives, and we don't think about it again until the next time we go to church. For most of us, these events happen on Palm Sunday and Easter. For some of us, we see them in the Masses of Holy Week – Palm Sunday, Holy Thursday, Good Friday, Holy Saturday, and Easter Sunday.

This year, I invite you to experience this week differently. These events are real. They are historical. They are shocking and devastating. They are surprising and exhilarating. In *Walking Through Holy Week*, you will see how each day allows us to enter into the action and be a part of the story. Imagine how different Easter will be when you experience the days leading up to it as the apostles did.

If we allow ourselves, we will feel the excitement of Jesus' entry into Jerusalem, and experience the wonder at the words of the Last Supper, when Jesus offers His body for the New Covenant. We will feel the horror and shock as Jesus is arrested, tried, and convicted. We will sense the darkness that descends as He dies on the cross. Then, as Easter comes, the light that pierces the darkness will be brighter than it ever was before. The ending we long for will arrive with the Resurrection. This will be a week like no other in the year. As it should be.

CHAPTER 1

Palm Sunday: Triumphal Entry to Tragic Ending

Sometimes the most promising of beginnings ends quickly in tragedy and leaves us wondering why. In 1986, Christa McCauliffe was going to be the first teacher in space. Schools around the country turned the televisions on during class for students to see this historic moment. There was more attention on this space shuttle launch than there had been in years. Spirits were high, and expectations were higher. As the shuttle lifted off, all seemed fine, and teachers were preparing to turn the program off and return to the school day. Suddenly, things went very wrong, and the shuttle exploded into fire and smoke, with the two booster rockets flying separately and alone into the distance. The hope and promise were gone in an instant, and the country was left wondering what had happened.

In our Palm Sunday Mass, we see that the Jewish people are in a very similar state. Hope and promise fill the day, but quickly things go very wrong. By the end of the week, their hopes are dashed with Jesus dead on the Cross, and they are left wondering how this could possibly have happened. Let us enter this Mass as one of those people. As you listen to the readings, put yourself in the scene, become one of the crowd, feel the exhilaration and the shock as they come. Be a part of this Mass as you never have before. You will not be disappointed.

Preparation

On a normal Sunday, my family and I arrive a few minutes (or sometimes a few seconds) early for Mass. As we sit in our seats, each one of us has our own way to prepare for Mass. Whether with a prayer, saying hello to friends around us, looking over the readings for the day, or looking at the song sheet to see if we recognize or like the music, we all get settled in so we can be present for the next hour or so. The music signals the beginning of the Mass, and we stand.

As we arrive on Palm Sunday, however, it is clear that this Mass is different. Visually, the somber purple of Lent has been replaced with red. Red on the vestments of the priest, red in the flowers, and maybe even red draped on the crucifix. When the Church wears red, it symbolizes the blood of sacrifice, whether it is the sacrifice of Jesus on the cross, or the sacrifice of martyrs who have given their lives for their faith. We are about to start joyfully, but we have an immediate reminder that this celebration is going to be short-lived. The clouds of sacrifice shadow the entry, and we begin.

> **WHAT HAPPENS TO THE PALMS AFTER PALM SUNDAY?**
> Traditionally, the leftover palms from Palm Sunday are burned and saved for the next Lenten season when we receive them on our foreheads as ashes on Ash Wednesday.

Entry

Matthew 21: 1-11

Most churches start Palm Sunday Mass outside of the sanctuary, and this is one of the few times of the year that the people in the congregation are given props. Each person is given a palm leaf, and we are suddenly, physically involved in the story. There is one more difference here. Before we even hear the entrance hymn, we jump into a Gospel story as a prelude.

We begin with the story of Jesus entering into Jerusalem to participate in the Passover feast. It is a triumphant entrance, with crowds of Jewish people ready for Jesus to step up as a leader. He is known as a prophet, and is hoped to be the Messiah – the one who will free them from the oppression of Rome and lead them as King. The Jews have been under Roman rule for more than sixty years, and while they were tolerated and allowed to practice their faith, there was a constant threat of being pressed into service, being imprisoned without cause, and being intimated with any number of acts of suppression. The hope of this moment is immense.

As you listen to this opening reading today, look at the crowds who have gathered, and feel the excitement and the anticipation. Enter into the story as you hold your palm at the ready, imagining the hope that stands before you, and joining in the "Hosanna" that is proclaimed. This man is a wonder-worker. This man is a prophet. This is the moment. The time has come. This is not some future promise for the Jewish people; it is the promise of freedom and restoration to a kingdom of their own, and it is right here in front of them. Hold your palm leaf and listen to the crowd. See how the whole city notices and wonders what is happening. They believe that change is coming, and it will be glorious. In that, they are correct.

■ *Matthew 21: 1-11* [1]

When Jesus and the disciples drew near Jerusalem and came to Bethphage on the Mount of Olives, Jesus sent two disciples, saying to them, "Go into the village opposite you, and immediately you will find an ass tethered, and a colt with her. Untie them and bring them here to me. And if anyone should say anything to you, reply, 'The master has need of them.' Then he will send them at once." This happened so that what had been spoken through the prophet might be fulfilled:

> Say to daughter Zion,
> "Behold, your king comes to you,
>   meek and riding on an ass,
>   and on a colt, the foal of a beast of burden." [2]

The disciples went and did as Jesus had ordered them. They brought the ass and the colt and laid their cloaks over them, and he sat upon them. The very large crowd spread their cloaks on the road, while others cut branches from the trees and strewed them on the road. The crowds preceding him and those following kept crying out and saying:

> "Hosanna to the Son of David;
>   blessed is he who comes in the name of the Lord;
> hosanna in the highest."

And when he entered Jerusalem the whole city was shaken and asked, "Who is this?" And the crowds replied, "This is Jesus the prophet, from Nazareth in Galilee."

---

[1] A FEW OF THE READINGS IN HOLY WEEK ROTATE EACH YEAR, BASED ON THE CYCLE OF READINGS. THOSE READINGS WILL BE NOTED WITH AN ASTERISK. YEAR A WILL BE INCLUDED IN THE TEXT, AND YEARS B AND C CAN BE FOUND IN APPENDIX A. THIS ENTRANCE GOSPEL (MATTHEW 21:1-11) IS FROM YEAR A.

[2] ISAIAH 62:11, ZECHARIAH 9:9

[3] THE TEXT FOR THESE VERSES ARE INCLUDED IN APPENDIX B

Did you notice when the Gospel said, "This happened so that what had been spoken through the prophet might be fulfilled?" Have you ever wondered who that prophet might be, and how the reader is supposed to know about it? This reference is a combination of two verses. Isaiah 62:11[3] and Zechariah 9:9, and would have been easily recognized by the Jewish people.

Both of these verses are parts of larger passages on the deliverance of Jerusalem from oppression, and the promise of a Messiah. Zechariah 9:9-13 describes the Messiah whom the people of Jerusalem were expecting.

Food for Thought

1. Read the passages from Isaiah and Zechariah 9 in Appendix B. After reading these scriptures, what would you have expected Jesus to do after he entered Jerusalem?

2. The Book of Zechariah continues with descriptions of battle and triumph, but changes suddenly from tales of success and glory to descriptions of grief and desolation. Read Zechariah 12:10-13:1, also located in Appendix B. What are some of the things that point to what Jesus is about to do?

3. Sometimes God allows things that don't make sense to us. Suffering, persecution, and failure can make us feel that God is not present, or doesn't care about us. Does this passage help you to see suffering differently or bring up more questions? Why?

First Reading

Isaiah 50:4-7

From this point on, the Palm Sunday Mass looks like every other Mass of the year. We open with prayer and move into the Old Testament reading. Just as in every other week, the Old Testament reading is directly linked to the Gospel. This week, the words we are about to hear, written hundreds of years before Jesus was even born, are prophetic. They tell us something true about who Jesus is and what He is doing. Chapters 49-55 of Isaiah are filled with descriptions that apply directly to the life of Jesus and the saving work He has come to accomplish. They are messages of hope and promises of salvation, yet at the very same moment they are descriptions of the suffering that must come with such a promise. Just as any overthrow of an oppressive government would be marked by much suffering and sacrifice, this salvation from the oppression of sin and death will come with a high cost.

The Scripture we read today comes directly from this Messianic part of Isaiah. Jesus has been given a mission to bring comfort to the weary. He is to give strength to those who falter, and He will not shy away from it. How comforting is this message? How wonderful to the ears of those who heard it? How comforting to us, knowing that it was meant for us to hear today?

- *Isaiah 50:4-7*

> *The Lord GOD has given me*
> *a well-trained tongue,*
> *that I might know how to speak to the weary*
> *a word that will rouse them.*
> *Morning after morning*
> *he opens my ear that I may hear;*
> *and I have not rebelled,*
> *have not turned back.*
> *I gave my back to those who beat me,*
> *my cheeks to those who plucked my beard;*
> *my face I did not shield*
> *from buffets and spitting.*

The Lord GOD is my help,
therefore I am not disgraced;
I have set my face like flint,
knowing that I shall not be put to shame.

As you listen to the first reading, can you hear the promise of fidelity? The word of salvation that Jesus speaks will be delivered, no matter the cost. This message is not only for the people of Israel, but for each one of us. Nothing will stop the love of God from coming through. Nothing. This message is delivered again and again, both in the Old Testament and in the New. The ugly face of death on a cross was not enough to deter Jesus from fulfilling His promise to us. We are worth anything He has to go through to get to us. Nothing we have done is bad enough to keep Him away. We can count on that.

At the same time, this reading reminds us that no matter what the world may put on us, no matter how shameful it may appear, if God is our help, there is no shame.

Death by crucifixion was one of the most public and shameful punishments that the Roman Empire could give. The criminals were on display for all to see and ridicule. It was long and unmerciful, and the people being executed were deemed worthy of such torture. The events to come may seem disgraceful to others, but God does not see things as the world does. There is much more to the picture than the shame and suffering that we are about see. It has been taken on so that we do not have to pay the cost of our sin. It is undeserved, but has been willingly accepted. Disgrace will be transformed into incredible grace. Because of our perspective, we know this much is true.

Food for Thought

1. Have you ever wanted to stand up for truth or your faith, but didn't do so because you might be ridiculed or teased? Have you stood up for truth and your faith, in spite of that risk?

2. In a challenging situation, we usually stand up for truth from a defensive position. If you did so in the spirit of this passage from Isaiah, knowing that you had a word that would rouse a weary soul, or that you could give grace to an ungraceful interaction, how might that change the situation?

Responsorial Psalm *Psalm 22:8-9, 17-18, 19-20, 23-24*

Between the Old Testament and the New Testament each week, we sing a Psalm. Growing up, I thought that this was just filler, and a way to get more of the Bible into the readings of the three-year cycle. Not surprisingly, I was wrong, and I discovered that the Psalm is usually directly related to the readings of the Mass.

For the Psalm and the New Testament reading today, we jump ahead of the story a bit and go to the cross. It seems a little out of place here, but it gives us perspective as we listen to the Gospel story later. This Psalm is particularly poignant. You'll recognize the antiphon or refrain right away – "My God, My God. Why have you abandoned me?" (Psalm 22:2). So often we see this as a sign of Jesus' feeling deserted by and separated from God. He cries out in despair and fear as He is dying on the cross.

How could this be? Jesus, who has been so close to His Father from the beginning, is now separated. Jesus, who has just come from the Garden, resolutely following the will of His Father, knowing that this is the cup He must drink, feels deserted at the moment that the plan is fulfilled. How does this make sense?

The people at the scene would have recognized the reference as Jesus called out from the cross, "My God, my God, why have you abandoned me?" The Scriptures were common knowledge, and just as "If you can't take the heat" would bring to our minds the rest of the phrase, "get out of the kitchen," this verse would have brought to mind the entire twenty-second Psalm. We only have parts of the twenty-second Psalm read at this Mass[1], but these parts are very telling of the statement that Jesus was making. He may have felt the separation from God that is caused by sin, and may have felt the abandonment required in the payment for that sin. But even in this, Jesus is expressing hope and trying to help us understand that God's work is being done here. There will be deliverance, but it will not be as expected.

■ *Psalm 22:8-9, 17-18, 19-20, 23-24*

R. (2a) My God, my God, why have you abandoned me?
All who see me scoff at me;
  they mock me with parted lips, they wag their heads:
"He relied on the LORD; let him deliver him,
  let him rescue him, if he loves him."

R. My God, my God, why have you abandoned me?
Indeed, many dogs surround me,
  a pack of evildoers closes in upon me;
They have pierced my hands and my feet;
  I can count all my bones.

R. My God, my God, why have you abandoned me?
They divide my garments among them,
  and for my vesture they cast lots.
But you, O LORD, be not far from me;
  O my help, hasten to aid me.

---

[1] FULL TEXT OF PSALM 22 IS LISTED IN APPENDIX B

R. My God, my God, why have you abandoned me?
I will proclaim your name to my brethren;
  in the midst of the assembly will I praise you:
"You who fear the LORD, praise him;
  all you descendants of Jacob, give glory to him;
  revere him, all you descendants of Israel!"

R. My God, my God, why have you abandoned me?

When we sing this Psalm, the prophecy of it is astounding. The first refrain we sing is almost a direct quote of those who mock Jesus on the cross in the readings of today's Gospel. The second refrain references the pierced hands and feet of the crucifixion. The third describes how Jesus' garments are gambled off when the soldiers cast lots for his tunic. We will hear all of these things before this Mass is over. Listen for them in the Gospel.

Finally, in the last refrain, we see that in the midst of all of this, the psalmist praises God. In the midst of this sacrifice, this suffering, this apparent failure, God is to be praised. Can you imagine hearing this from a man hanging from a cross? Put yourself in that moment, and see this person, beaten beyond recognition, telling you that all is not as it seems. There is something more here than meets the eye. There is work being done that the people present could not possibly have understood. Even now, it is hard for us to understand. But in these few words, Jesus is telling us that all of this was in the plan. This was known from the beginning, and God is worthy of our praise within it.

Even in this, Jesus is expressing hope and trying to help us understand that God's work is being done. There will be deliverance, but it will not be as expected

Food for Thought

1. How do you think Jesus' suffering could be a part of God's plan for salvation?

2. Have you ever seen suffering bring about a blessing or a positive change? What was it?

Second Reading *Philippians 2:6-11*

The second reading of Mass is always from the New Testament. While the Gospels tell of the life of Jesus, the remaining books pick up the story after Jesus returns to heaven. They tell the story of the beginnings of the church and help Jesus' followers to understand who Jesus was, what He did, and how we are to live in a way consistent with that truth.

■ *Philippians 2:6-11*

Christ Jesus, though he was in the form of God,
did not regard equality with God
something to be grasped.
Rather, he emptied himself,
taking the form of a slave,
coming in human likeness;
and found human in appearance,
he humbled himself,
becoming obedient to the point of death,
even death on a cross.

> *Because of this, God greatly exalted him*
> *and bestowed upon him the name*
> *which is above every name,*
> *that at the name of Jesus*
> *every knee should bend,*
> *of those in heaven and on earth and under the earth,*
> *and every tongue confess that*
> *Jesus Christ is Lord,*
> *to the glory of God the Father.*

This reading from Philippians tells us the whole story in a short paragraph. Jesus came. He was God, but it didn't matter to Him. He didn't want to live as God; instead, He wanted to be like us. He wanted to show us how to live a life of obedience, and He followed God's will for Him all the way to the end. Shortly, we will read the Gospel, and we will leave this Mass in the darkest moment of our salvation story. This reading helps us to remember that there is more to come. This cost is small compared to the return that it brings. Soon all heaven and earth will know who Jesus is and what He has done for us. This is our Lord. Hold on to it. Remember.

Food for Thought

1. This reading describes Jesus in two ways – humble servant and powerful ruler. Which of these descriptions speaks to you right now?

2. How does that affect the way you approach Easter this year?

Gospel *Matthew 26:14-27:66 (short version Matthew 27:11-54)*

The Gospel readings for Palm Sunday are read on a three-year rotation. Each year, we will hear a slightly different version, but all of them will go through the Passover, the agony in the garden, the arrest and trial of Jesus, and finally through the crucifixion. This is our preview of the days to come in Holy Week.

The Gospel today is like a movie preview of Holy Week. As with any movie preview, we can see the story and understand much of what will happen within it. However, when we watch it again after seeing the entire movie, we have a deeper understanding and better perspective for each of the short scenes that we saw in the preview. After you go through this entire Holy Week, come back here and see how much more you find in the story being told today.

For the rest of Holy Week, each one of the days mentioned in today's Gospel will be played out as they come. On Thursday, we will attend the Last Supper with Jesus as He celebrates the Passover with His disciples, then go into the garden with Him to pray on Friday, we will go from the garden to Jesus' arrest, trial, and crucifixion on Saturday, we will wait. Each day's service will bring us deeply into the narrative, but for today, we walk through the events quickly.

(In the short versions of the Gospel reading, the events of Holy Week are left out. Instead, the readings go directly to the trial and crucifixion of Jesus.)

As we read the Gospel today, it is shocking how quickly we move from celebration to despair, from triumph to tragedy. It may seem that the accounts have been condensed to fit conveniently into a week's celebration for Easter, but biblically, this timeline is decidedly accurate. Jesus arrives in Jerusalem at the beginning of the week in triumph, and by Thursday, the tables have turned dramatically. We are reminded in short order as we read the Gospel, that we are a fickle people, easily swayed by the crowds, and easily moved from truth that doesn't look like we expect it to be.

I used to listen to this Gospel thinking that I would never do something as cruel as calling for the death of a man I had so recently welcomed with such joy. I would never succumb to the pressure of the crowds, and surely I

> *I was angry, scared, and hurt, and wanted nothing to do with this God who would allow such things to happen. God hadn't tuned His back on me. I had turned my back on Him.*

would stand up for Jesus. "They" were so misled and easily swayed. "They" were blind and fickle.

Then one day, after sitting with this reading, I realized that this is not the story of "them," but the story of "us." I realized that I was fickle. I saw that when things were going well for me, I could praise God easily for the blessings I received. If things went according to my plan, I could easily give God the credit and the glory. However, as soon as heartbreak hit, or as soon as tragedy struck, I threw Him right out. Me. The one who writes Bible studies and an inspirational blog. Absolutely.

I remember standing in my ten-year-old daughter's room in the ER as she was waiting for an assessment of her badly broken arm. This was her third broken bone in two years, and the break was in the exact same place as the one just months before. However, this one was much, much worse. On the way in, her heart was beating in an irregular way, and the paramedic in the ambulance recommended that we check that once we got to the ER. One of the worst things in that room was the constant beeping of the monitors, and especially the irregular beeping and alarm bells on the heart monitor that she was wearing. Everything about this moment was pointing to a difficult future filled with heart problems and brittle bones, and I wanted none of it.

I was angry, scared, and hurt, and I wanted nothing to do with this God who would allow such things to happen. In this moment, I was pretty sure that He had abandoned us, or even worse, that He was allowing or causing this pain and potential suffering to happen. This is not the God I wanted or expected, and I told Him so. I stood right there in that room and prayed, "God, I do not want to go where you are leading me. I will not listen, and I will not go."

At a moment like this, there would have been no way that I would stand up for Jesus in a crowd of angry people. I didn't want this kind of a Savior. I preferred someone who would fight for me, and promised a life of safety and freedom. The problem is that when I turned from God and refused even to enter into His presence in this moment, I missed the opportunity for Him to minister to me in my suffering. I missed the opportunity to see the blessings that were coming to my daughter as she suffered. I missed all of the moments when I was told, "Do not be afraid. I am not giving you the cross that you are anticipating." I missed the opportunity to help my daughter hear the same thing, and I distanced myself from God in a way that took many months to recover. God hadn't turned His back on me. I turned my back on Him.

Consequently, we can see that the Jewish people in the story are not so different from us after all. On Palm Sunday, they welcomed their Savior, ready to crown their King and throw off the oppression of the Romans. Jesus spent four days in the Temple, teaching and answering questions and challenges. He was closely scrutinized and intensely investigated. The more He taught, the more they saw that this was not who they expected. By the end of the examination, the verdict had been reached. This man was not their Savior.

As we read the Gospel today, place yourself in the story. Sit with Jesus at dinner. Follow Him to the garden, and watch His arrest. Go into the courtyard with the crowds calling for Barabbas to be freed. Even if you believed Jesus was the Messiah, what would you have thought as He stood in front of you, beaten within an inch of His life? Would you have gone against the crowd and called for His release? Would you have stood up for this man who didn't seem to have the strength to stand up to Pilate? Would you put your life on the line for Him? Listen closely to the reading, and see yourself in the story. I imagine you're not as different from the crowd as you thought.

■ *Matthew 26:14-27:66* [1]

One of the Twelve, who was called Judas Iscariot, went to the chief priests and said, "What are you willing to give me if I hand him over to you?" They paid him thirty pieces of silver, and from that time on he looked for an opportunity to hand him over.

On the first day of the Feast of Unleavened Bread, the disciples approached Jesus and said,

"Where do you want us to prepare for you to eat the Passover?" He said, "Go into the city to a certain man and tell him, 'The teacher says, "My appointed time draws near; in your house I shall celebrate the Passover with my disciples."'" The disciples then did as Jesus had ordered, and prepared the Passover.

When it was evening, he reclined at table with the Twelve. And while they were eating, he said, "Amen, I say to you, one of you will betray me." Deeply distressed at this, they began to say to him one after another, "Surely it is not I, Lord?" He said in reply, "He who has dipped his hand into the dish with me is the one who will betray me. The Son of Man indeed goes, as it is written of him, but woe to that man by whom the Son of Man is betrayed. It would be better for that man if he had never been born." Then Judas, his betrayer, said in reply, "Surely it is not I, Rabbi?" He answered, "You have said so."

While they were eating, Jesus took bread, said the blessing, broke it, and giving it to his disciples said, "Take and eat; this is my body." Then he took a cup, gave thanks, and gave it to them, saying, "Drink from it, all of you, for this is my blood of the covenant, which will be shed on behalf of many for the forgiveness of sins. I tell you, from now on I shall not drink this fruit of the vine until the day when I drink it with you new in the kingdom of my Father." Then, after singing a hymn, they went out to the Mount of Olives.

---

[1] READINGS FOR YEARS B AND C ARE FOUND IN APPENDIX A

Then Jesus said to them, "This night all of you will have your faith in me shaken, for it is written:

> I will strike the shepherd,
>   and the sheep of the flock will be dispersed;

but after I have been raised up, I shall go before you to Galilee." Peter said to him in reply, "Though all may have their faith in you shaken, mine will never be." Jesus said to him, "Amen, I say to you, this very night before the cock crows, you will deny me three times." Peter said to him, "Even though I should have to die with you, I will not deny you." And all the disciples spoke likewise.

Then Jesus came with them to a place called Gethsemane, and he said to his disciples, "Sit here while I go over there and pray." He took along Peter and the two sons of Zebedee, and began to feel sorrow and distress. Then he said to them, "My soul is sorrowful even to death. Remain here and keep watch with me." He advanced a little and fell prostrate in prayer, saying, "My Father, if it is possible, let this cup pass from me; yet, not as I will, but as you will." When he returned to his disciples he found them asleep. He said to Peter, "So you could not keep watch with me for one hour? Watch and pray that you may not undergo the test. The spirit is willing, but the flesh is weak." Withdrawing a second time, he prayed again, "My Father, if it is not possible that this cup pass without my drinking it, your will be done!"

Jesus took the bread, said the blessing broke it, and giving it to his disciples said, "Take and eat; this is my body"

Then he returned once more and found them asleep, for they could not keep their eyes open. He left them and withdrew again and prayed a third time, saying the same thing again. Then he returned to his disciples and said to them, "Are you still sleeping and taking your rest? Behold, the hour is at hand when the Son of Man is to be handed over to sinners. Get up, let us go. Look, my betrayer is at hand."

While he was still speaking, Judas, one of the Twelve, arrived, accompanied by a large crowd, with swords and clubs, who had come from the chief priests and the elders of the people. His betrayer had arranged a sign with them, saying, "The man I shall kiss is the one; arrest him." Immediately he went over to Jesus and said, "Hail, Rabbi!" and he kissed him. Jesus answered him, "Friend, do what you have come for." Then stepping forward they laid hands on Jesus and arrested him. And behold, one of those who accompanied Jesus put his hand to his sword, drew it, and struck the high priest's servant, cutting off his ear. Then Jesus said to him, "Put your sword back into its sheath, for all who take the sword will perish by the sword. Do you think that I cannot call upon my Father and he will not provide me at this moment with more than twelve legions of angels? But then how would the Scriptures be fulfilled which say that it must come to pass in this way?" At that hour Jesus said to the crowds, "Have you come out as against a robber, with swords and clubs to seize me? Day after day I sat teaching in the temple area, yet you did not arrest me. But all this has come to pass that the writings of the prophets may be fulfilled." Then all the disciples left him and fled.

Those who had arrested Jesus led him away to Caiaphas the high priest, where the scribes and the elders were assembled. Peter was following him at a distance as far as the high priest's courtyard, and going inside he sat down with the servants to see the outcome. The chief priests and the entire Sanhedrin kept trying to obtain false testimony against Jesus in order to put him to death, but they found none, though many false witnesses came forward. Finally two came forward who stated, "This man said, 'I can destroy the temple of God and within three days rebuild it.'" The high priest rose and addressed

> *Behold, the hour is at hand when the Son of Man is to be handed over to sinners. Get up, let us go. Look, my betrayer is at hand.*

him, "Have you no answer? What are these men testifying against you?" But Jesus was silent. Then the high priest said to him, "I order you to tell us under oath before the living God whether you are the Christ, the Son of God." Jesus said to him in reply, "You have said so. But I tell you:

> From now on you will see 'the Son of Man
> seated at the right hand of the Power'
> and 'coming on the clouds of heaven.'"

Then the high priest tore his robes and said, "He has blasphemed! What further need have we of witnesses? You have now heard the blasphemy; what is your opinion?" They said in reply, "He deserves to die!" Then they spat in his face and struck him, while some slapped him, saying, "Prophesy for us, Christ: who is it that struck you?" Now Peter was sitting outside in the courtyard. One of the maids came over to him and said, "You too were with Jesus the Galilean." But he denied it in front of everyone, saying, "I do not know what you are talking about!" As he went out to the gate, another girl saw him and said to those who were there, "This man was with Jesus the Nazorean." Again he denied it with an oath, "I do not know the man!" A little later the bystanders came over and said to Peter, "Surely you too are one of them; even your speech gives you away." At that he began to curse and to swear, "I do not know the man." And immediately a cock crowed. Then Peter remembered the word that Jesus had spoken: "Before the cock crows you will deny me three times." He went out and began to weep bitterly.

When it was morning, all the chief priests and the elders of the people took counsel against Jesus to put him to death. They bound him, led him away, and handed him over to Pilate, the governor.

Then Judas, his betrayer, seeing that Jesus had been condemned, deeply regretted what he had done. He returned the thirty pieces of silver to the chief priests and elders, saying, "I have sinned in betraying innocent blood." They said, "What is that to us? Look to it yourself." Flinging the money into the temple, he departed and went off and hanged himself. The chief priests gathered up the money, but said, "It is not lawful to deposit this in the temple treasury, for it is the price of blood." After consultation, they used it to buy the potter's field as a burial place for foreigners. That is why that field even today is called the Field of Blood. Then was fulfilled what had been said through Jeremiah the prophet, And they took the thirty pieces of silver, the value of a man with a price on his head, a price set by some of the Israelites, and they paid it out for the potter's field just as the Lord had commanded me.

> # Now Jesus stood before the governor, and he questioned him, "Are you the king of the Jews?" Jesus said, "You say so."

Now Jesus stood before the governor, and he questioned him, "Are you the king of the Jews?" Jesus said, "You say so." And when he was accused by the chief priests and elders, he made no answer. Then Pilate said to him, "Do you not hear how many things they are testifying against you?" But he did not answer him one word, so that the governor was greatly amazed.

"Which one do you want me to release to you, Barabbas, or Jesus called Christ?" They answered, "Barabbas!"

Now on the occasion of the feast the governor was accustomed to release to the crowd one prisoner whom they wished. And at that time they had a notorious prisoner called Barabbas. So when they had assembled, Pilate said to them, "Which one do you want me to release to you, Barabbas, or Jesus called Christ?" For he knew that it was out of envy that they had handed him over. While he was still seated on the bench, his wife sent him a message, "Have nothing to do with that righteous man. I suffered much in a dream today because of him." The chief priests and the elders persuaded the crowds to ask for Barabbas but to destroy Jesus. The governor said to them in reply, "Which of the two do you want me to release to you?" They answered, "Barabbas!" Pilate said to them, "Then what shall I do with Jesus called Christ?" They all said, "Let him be crucified!" But he said, "Why? What evil has he done?" They only shouted the louder, "Let him be crucified!" When Pilate saw that he was not succeeding at all, but that a riot was breaking out instead, he took water and washed his hands in the sight of the crowd, saying, "I am innocent of this man's blood. Look to it yourselves." And the whole people said in reply, "His blood be upon us and upon our children." Then he released Barabbas to them, but after he had Jesus scourged, he handed him over to be crucified.

Then the soldiers of the governor took Jesus inside the praetorium and gathered the whole cohort around him. They stripped off his clothes and threw a scarlet military cloak about him. Weaving a crown out of thorns, they placed it on his head, and a reed in his right hand. And kneeling before him, they mocked him, saying, "Hail, King of the Jews!" They spat upon him and took the reed and kept striking him on the head. And when they had mocked him, they stripped him of the cloak, dressed him in his own clothes, and led him off to crucify him.

And at about three o'clock Jesus cried out in a loud voice, "Eli, Eli, lema sabachthani?" which means, "My God, my God why have you forsaken me?"

As they were going out, they met a Cyrenian named Simon; this man they pressed into service to carry his cross.

And when they came to a place called Golgotha —which means Place of the Skull —, they gave Jesus wine to drink mixed with gall. But when he had tasted it, he refused to drink. After they had crucified him, they divided his garments by casting lots; then they sat down and kept watch over him there. And they placed over his head the written charge against him: This is Jesus, the King of the Jews. Two revolutionaries were crucified with him, one on his right and the other on his left. Those passing by reviled him, shaking their heads and saying, "You who would destroy the temple and rebuild it in three days, save yourself, if you are the Son of God, and come down from the cross!" Likewise the chief priests with the scribes and elders mocked him and said, "He saved others; he cannot save himself. So he is the king of Israel! Let him come down from the cross now, and we will believe in him. He trusted in God; let him deliver him now if he wants him. For he said, 'I am the Son of God.'" The revolutionaries who were crucified with him also kept abusing him in the same way.

From noon onward, darkness came over the whole land until three in the afternoon. And about three o'clock Jesus cried out in a loud voice, "Eli, Eli, lema sabachthani?" which means, "My God, my God, why have you forsaken me?" Some of the bystanders who heard it said, "This one is calling for Elijah." Immediately one of them ran to get a sponge; he soaked it in wine, and putting it on a reed, gave it to him to drink. But the rest said, "Wait, let us see if Elijah comes to save him." But Jesus cried out again in a loud voice, and gave up his spirit.

And behold, the veil of the sanctuary was torn in two from top to bottom. The earth quaked, rocks were split, tombs were opened, and the bodies of many saints who had fallen asleep were raised. And coming forth from their tombs after his resurrection, they entered the holy city and appeared to many. The centurion and the men with him who were keeping watch over Jesus feared greatly when they saw the earthquake and all that was happening, and they said, "Truly, this was the Son of God!" There were many women there, looking on from a distance, who had followed Jesus from Galilee, ministering to him. Among them were Mary Magdalene and Mary the mother of James and Joseph, and the mother of the sons of Zebedee.

When it was evening, there came a rich man from Arimathea named Joseph, who was himself a disciple of Jesus. He went to Pilate and asked for the body of Jesus; then Pilate ordered it to be handed over. Taking the body, Joseph wrapped it in clean linen and laid it in his new tomb that he had hewn in the rock. Then he rolled a huge stone across the entrance to the tomb and departed. But Mary Magdalene and the other Mary remained sitting there, facing the tomb.

The next day, the one following the day of preparation, the chief priests and the Pharisees gathered before Pilate and said, "Sir, we remember that this impostor while still alive said, 'After three days I will be raised up.' Give orders, then, that the grave be secured until the third day, lest his disciples come and steal him and say to the people, 'He has been raised from the dead.' This last imposture would be worse than the first." Pilate said to them, "The guard is yours; go, secure it as best you can." So they went and secured the tomb by fixing a seal to the stone and setting the guard.

It's a crazy dichotomy: the ones who understand Jesus the most, believe Him the least.

There are many things in this Gospel that will be explored in the coming chapters. For now, let's look at a couple of interesting points that we'll want to keep in mind as we journey through Holy Week.

When Jesus tells the disciples that they will fulfill Scripture when they scatter and abandon Him, He immediately follows the statement by saying, "but after I have been raised up, I shall go before you to Galilee." (Matthew 26:32). Jesus has already moved past the failure of the disciples and is preparing them for His return. However, just as we have heard this every year, and probably missed it, the disciples missed it, too. They focus on denying the fact that they will abandon Jesus. Rather than face their weakness and see the promise offered to them, they miss it completely and are lost and confused as their Savior dies on the cross.

In contrast, the people who are convinced that Jesus is a fraud and blasphemer understand exactly what Jesus is saying. The chief priests and Pharisees ask Pilate to secure the tomb, because Jesus had claimed that He would rise again after three days. It's a crazy dichotomy: the ones who understand Jesus the most, believe Him the least. There will be many more of these moments in the days to come. Watch for them.

Food for Thought

1. When you hear this reading at Mass, you are standing with a palm leaf in hand, listening to the events as they unfold before you. How would you react in the courtyard with the crowds calling for the death of Jesus?

2. As this reading comes to a close, what are you thinking? What do you feel?

3. How does it set the tone for the coming days of Holy Week?

The rest of the Mass continues as it usually does each Sunday. At the end, we leave in song, knowing that this week has just begun. Easter is coming, but there is much to do before it gets here. We will come back on Holy Thursday to pick it back up again.

Mass Moments

In each lesson, there will be some things that stand out for you. It may be a new insight, it may be a way you want to engage more purposefully as you participate in the Mass, or it may be some detail that you didn't know about that you want to watch for. At the end of the book, I have provided you with a cheat sheet of sorts. Fill in the things you want to remember for each Mass in Holy Week. Then when Holy Week arrives, review your notes, and take them with you to Mass. I promise it will be a different experience this year.

MAKING A PALM CROSS

1. Take a palm leaf and fold it over, creasing it about a fourth of the way up from the bottom. The top of the leaf should be behind the bottom of the leaf. The wider, bottom part of the leaf will form the base of the cross.

2. Fold the back leaf 90 degrees to one side about ⅓ of the way down the base of the cross to start creating the cross-beam. Crease the angled fold behind the base.

3. Fold the cross-beam back over the top of the base of the cross, and press the edge of the beam.

4. Fold the cross-beam back again, creating the full cross-beam and returning the leaf behind the base of the cross.

5. Fold the leaf diagonally, and wrap it around the point where the base and the cross-beam connect. This will hold the two pieces together.

6. Wrap around again, crossing over in the other direction to make a small x at the center of the cross-beam.

7. Repeat if needed, and tuck the end of the palm leave into the back of the cross you have created, trimming any extra or wrapping it around until the leaf has been used completely.

CHAPTER 2

Holy Thursday: The Passover Transformed

Holy Thursday has long been a day of debate in our family. Officially, Lent is over, and we move into what is called the Triduum. At issue is whether chocolate, coffee, Netflix, or whatever else has been given up for the last 40 days is available for guilt-free consumption. Some say that Lent is over, so there is no more need to wait. Others in the family say that Lent may be over, but Easter hasn't arrived, so the waiting should and must continue. Even the priests we ask to help us solve our dilemma step clear of the quagmire and tell us to follow our consciences. I'm sure there will be another round of accusatory glances this year as some in the family trot out their treats before the Easter bunny has had a chance to deliver them.

Preparation

And so we begin. Holy Thursday opens the Triduum, a Latin word meaning "three days." As we go through Holy Thursday, Good Friday, and Holy Saturday or the Easter Vigil, notice that they are all one Mass. We will enter on Thursday with song, and an opening prayer, but we will not close. We will not be dismissed with the command to "Go and spread the Gospel" or any other words of sending. We will leave, only to return and pick up a little later in the story. The dismissal will not come until Saturday night, because each of these days is a pivotal part of what is happening. None of them can stand alone without the others. Each night, we leave and wait, just as the disciples did. There was little sleep in those days for the people in the story. There was no break in the relentless progress of the machine bringing Jesus to the cross. There will be no stopping for us either.

Entry

The priest walks into this Mass dressed in white. These are the vestments of Easter, and they seem out of place here. As I said before, there is some debate in my family on when Lent is over, and how the days before Easter fit in. The start of the Triduum is equally confusing - what are these vestments doing here?

Today we celebrate the institution of the Eucharist. This is the moment when Jesus lets us in on the plan and gives us the way to participate in it for all time. It is the moment that He gives us a way to receive Him that goes far beyond any gift we have ever received before. The vestments are white because this is a joyous celebration. They are white because Jesus is with us always. He will never leave.

There is something else odd here as we enter the church. The Tabernacle, which holds the Blessed Sacrament, is open and empty. Today begins the process of Jesus being removed from our sight. We will receive Him today in the transformed bread and wine, but then He will leave for the garden and HE will be taken from us. The Blessed Sacrament will be reposed elsewhere, out of view, and will not return to the tabernacle until Saturday night.

The tabernacle, which holds the Blessed Sacrament, is open and empty. Today begins the process of Jesus being removed from our sight

Incense

As part of the entrance procession, the priest will incense the altar to prepare it for this most solemn of celebrations. The smoke of the incense traditionally represents the prayers of the faithful rising to heaven. As it is used at various times during the Triduum liturgy, the purpose is to purify and bless that which is being incensed.

> *Let my prayer be incense before you;*
> *my uplifted hands an evening offering (Psalm 141:2)*

> *For we are the aroma of Christ for God among those who are being saved and among those who are perishing. (2 Cor 2:15)*

The incense will also be used as the Gospel is read, as the gifts are brought to the altar, over the people in the congregation, and to prepare the altar before the Consecration, when the bread and wine are transformed into the body and blood of Christ. It will be used several times over the next few days. These moments signal to us that something important and blessed is present or is about to happen, and we lift our prayers heavenward as we participate in them.

Gloria

As we begin the Mass there is another moment that seems to be out of place. In the somberness of Lent, we have only sung the Gloria at two masses: the Solemnities of St. Joseph and of the Annunciation. We have not sung the Alleluia at all. While we still refrain from singing Alleluia, we start this Mass with bells ringing and Gloria ringing from the rafters. We sing as the angels did when Jesus was born,

> "Glory to God in the highest
> and on earth peace to those on whom his favor rests." (Luke 2:14)

The rest of the Gloria is a type of creed, or statement of belief, which reminds us that the events of Easter cannot be separated from the beginning of the story. This Holy Week has been the plan all along, and the Savior was recognized at the moment of His birth. It was foretold by John the Baptist as Jesus' public ministry began: "Behold, the Lamb of God, who takes away the sin of the world." (John 1:29b). And it was seen after the resurrection by Stephen as he was martyred for his faith: "But [Stephen], filled with the holy Spirit, looked up intently to heaven and saw the glory of Jesus standing at the right hand of God, and he said, 'Behold, I see the heavens opened and the Son of Man standing at the right hand of God.'" (Acts 7:55-56) After the Gloria is sung, the bells will again go silent until they announce the resurrection of the Lord on Saturday night.

> *Glory to God in the highest, and on earth peace, peace to people of good will. We praise you, we bless you, we adore you, we glorify you. We give you thanks for your great glory. Lord, God, heavenly King, O God, almighty Father.*
>
> *Lord, Jesus Christ, only begotten Son, Lord God, Lamb of God, Son of the Father, you take away the sins of the world, have mercy on us. You take away the sins of the world, receive our prayer. You are seated at the right hand of the Father, have mercy on us. For you alone are the Holy One, you alone are the Lord, you alone are the Most High, Jesus Christ, with the Holy Spirit, in the glory of God the father. Amen.*

First Reading

Exodus 12:1-8, 11-14

St. Augustine says, "The New Testament lies hidden in the Old, and the Old Testament is unveiled in the New." We cannot separate the two; they are intrinsically connected. While the Old Testament carries a story in its own right, each of these moments points to some greater reality that is revealed in the New Testament. David's kingship over a nation is fulfilled in the kingship of Jesus over all of us. In the waters of baptism, the Holy Spirit fulfills the cleansing waters of Noah's flood and the Red Sea of the Exodus. Our first reading is filled with these points of anticipation and fulfillment. We start our walk through the Triduum in Egypt. As we do, watch for the moments that point to Jesus and to the work that He is about to do.

> ■ *Exodus 12:1-8, 11-14*
>
> *The LORD said to Moses and Aaron in the land of Egypt, "This month shall stand at the head of your calendar; you shall reckon it the first month of the year. Tell the whole community of Israel: On the tenth of this month every one of your families must procure for itself a lamb, one apiece for each household. If a family is too small for a whole lamb, it shall join the nearest household in procuring one and shall share in the lamb in proportion to the number of persons who partake of it. The lamb must be a year-old male and without blemish. You may take it from either the sheep or the goats. You shall keep it until the fourteenth day of this month, and then, with the whole assembly of Israel present, it shall be slaughtered during the evening twilight. They shall take some of its blood and apply it to the two doorposts and the lintel of every house in which they partake of the lamb. That same night they shall eat its roasted flesh with unleavened bread and bitter herbs.*
>
> *"This is how you are to eat it: with your loins girt, sandals on your feet and your staff in hand, you shall eat like those who are in flight. It is the Passover of the LORD. For on this same night I will go through Egypt, striking down every firstborn of the land, both man and beast, and executing judgment on all the gods of Egypt—I, the LORD! But the blood will mark the houses where you are. Seeing the blood, I will pass over you; thus, when I strike the land of Egypt, no destructive blow will come upon you.*

> *"This day shall be a memorial feast for you, which all your generations shall celebrate with pilgrimage to the LORD, as a perpetual institution."*

Passover is a Jewish feast celebrating the deliverance of the Israelites from slavery in Egypt. It's a story that most of us know well. Moses asks Pharaoh to allow the Israelites to leave so they can worship their God. Of course, Pharaoh says no, and God begins to send plagues upon the Egyptian people. The tenth and final plague is the worst. The angel of death will come at night to kill all of the firstborn sons in the land.

God tells the Israelite people to prepare. This will be the point of departure, and they have to be ready to leave. Before they go, they have to protect themselves and show their faithfulness. The Israelites are to prepare a sacrifice for the night of the plague, and here is where the parallels with Jesus begin. Each family must procure a lamb, spotless and without blemish. It must be a perfect lamb, and they must spend four days with it to examine it and be sure. Coincidentally, Jesus arrived in Jerusalem on Sunday–four days ago–and He has been teaching and speaking in and around the Temple ever since. The religious leaders ask Jesus to tell them who gave Him the authority to teach.[1] They try to trap Jesus with questions about paying taxes, the resurrection, and the Law.[2] This Lamb of God has been closely scrutinized, and it is time to move to the next step.

In the Passover meal, the lamb is to be slaughtered and eaten, but first each family must paint the blood of this perfect lamb on the frame of the door with a hyssop branch.[3] In the Old Testament, blood was very important. It was the carrier of life and was treated with the utmost respect and dignity. In this sacrifice, the blood of the lamb symbolized the life that was given in place of the life required by the angel of death who would come that night. From our perspective, this would seem to be enough. The symbolic act is complete, the symbol has been applied to the door, and it is time to continue on with our lives.

---

[1] MATTHEW 21:23

[2] MATTHEW 22:15-40

[3] NOTE THE USE OF HYSSOP TO PAINT THE BLOOD ON THE DOOR. THIS WILL COME INTO PLAY AT THE CROSS.

In many sacrifices, this blood was placed on the altar, and the meat was burned so the smoke rose to heaven as a fragrant offering. The action was all that was needed. However, the Passover sacrifice was different. Offering the blood of the lamb was not nearly enough. This was not an offering simply to be given to the Lord, but a sacrifice of communion where each person was required to participate in a very intimate way. The lamb had to be consumed, and consumed completely. No one would be left untouched, and the lamb would not only be used to mark the doors of the faithful visibly, but would be within each one of them literally. Each of them would be marked, the angel of death would pass over, and they would be saved from death and slavery.

We, too, will participate in this sacrifice, but not until it has been changed in a surprising way.

Food for Thought

1. Given that the Israelites were about to flee with very little notice (they wouldn't even have time to allow their bread to rise), there is an additional benefit to this sacrifice of communion. Not only do they fully participate in the sacrifice, but they are also given sustenance for the journey they are about to undertake. What do you think they could expect from God in the days to come?

2. Do you have a time that God prepared you to leave a place of difficulty or suffering? How did He get you ready?

> **BE CAREFUL WHAT YOU SAY...**
>
> I taught this Holy Thursday lesson to a group of families one year, and I learned that you have to be careful with your presentation. To help the children understand the story, I asked the group to raise their hands if they were the firstborn child. "If you are a boy," I continued, "you would be killed on this night." Small pause to let this sink in. "But, you are lucky. Your parents believe in God, and He has told them what to do." I then continued with the story of the Passover lamb and the blood, and had them draw and color their own houses as if there was blood on the doorframe.
>
> The next day, the kindergarten teacher called me concerned about a conversation between my daughter, Lindsey, and her friend:
>
> Lindsey: **Avery, is your brother Michael the oldest?**
>
> Avery: **Yes.**
>
> Lindsey: **Then he's going to die tonight.**
>
> Avery looks up slightly confused, shrugs her shoulders, says, "Hmm," and goes right back into her coloring. End of conversation.
>
> After a quick explanation to the teacher, all was back in order, and her worries were put to rest. We thought it funny that poor Michael's sister didn't seem the least bit concerned about his impending demise. Sibling love...

Responsorial Psalm *Psalm 116: 12-13, 15-16BC, 17-18*

There are four cups of wine in the celebration of a Passover meal. The first cup is the cup of sanctification, and the prayer over it expresses the sanctity of the Sabbath. The second is presented with the story of the Exodus and the delivery of God's people from slavery. The third cup is offered in thanksgiving with a prayer of grace over the meal. Finally, the last cup is known as the blessing-cup, and it is offered with psalms and songs of praise. This last cup is one that acknowledges the blessings that have come because of the deliverance that God has given.

In the Response for the Psalm for today, we sing of the blessing-cup, and we are reminded of the wine that is offered in praise of the deliverance from slavery and death. We sing of communion, and we are reminded that we become a part of the sacrifice. As we sing of the Blood of Christ, we are reminded that the blood of salvation comes not from a lamb, but instead from The Lamb of God. This is how we are to participate; this is how we are to be freed.

The Response for this Psalm is not actually taken from the Psalm itself but is taken from 1 Corinthians 10:16 in order to give us the context in which to interpret the Psalm that we sing. The verses take on an entirely different meaning when placed in this context. Knowing what is coming, see how the phrases change and tell so much more of the story than we would have known if we were present at the Last Supper.

■ *Psalm 116: 12-13, 15-16BC, 17-18*

R. (cf. 1 Cor 10:16) Our blessing-cup is a communion with the Blood of Christ.
How shall I make a return to the LORD
    for all the good he has done for me?
The cup of salvation I will take up,
    and I will call upon the name of the LORD.
R. Our blessing-cup is a communion with the Blood of Christ.
Precious in the eyes of the LORD
    is the death of his faithful ones.
I am your servant, the son of your handmaid;
    you have loosed my bonds.
R. Our blessing-cup is a communion with the Blood of Christ.
To you will I offer sacrifice of thanksgiving,
    and I will call upon the name of the LORD.
My vows to the LORD I will pay
    in the presence of all his people.
R. Our blessing-cup is a communion with the Blood of Christ.

All of these verses were written hundreds of years before Jesus was even born, but as we read, we can see that each one of them is very telling of the work being done through Him in this moment. First, the response tells us that the cup that Jesus will raise is one of salvation. At the beginning of His ministry, Jesus changed the water into wine at the Wedding in Cana. Today, He will change the wine of the Passover or Seder meal and will show us that this cup of salvation is to become the cup of His blood. We are reminded of His words, "Drink from it, all of you, for this is my blood of the covenant, which will be shed on behalf of many for the forgiveness of sins." (Matthew 26:27-28) Later, in the garden, Jesus will ask for this cup to be taken from Him, and the answer will be "no." The blood of the lamb is no longer on the doorpost, but part of our Eucharistic sacrifice of communion.

The second refrain reveals that Jesus' death is precious. There is something valuable here, and the Psalm points us to it. We rarely think of the death of someone holy as something that could be precious in the eyes of the LORD, but here we are told that it is.

> *As we sing of the Blood of Christ, we are reminded that the blood of salvation comes not from a lamb, but instead from The Lamb of God. This is how we are to participate, this is how we are to be freed.*

As the refrain continues, we realize that Jesus is intended here when it says, "I am your servant, the son of your handmaid." When Mary agrees to God's plan for her to give birth to the Savior, her response starts with, "I am the handmaid of the Lord." (Luke 1:38a) Who would be the son of God's handmaid referred to in the Psalm? Jesus.

In our last refrain, we see that this Passover celebration is one of thanksgiving. The Israelites have been freed from slavery and death in Egypt, and they are celebrating by remembering what God has done for them. The word Eucharist comes from a Greek word meaning "thanksgiving" and reminds us that our celebration each week is to be filled with gratitude. However, this refrain informs us that this is not a feast of thanksgiving, but a sacrifice of thanksgiving. Our sin will be on display soon, in an ugly and brutal way. The cost will be paid for us through the sacrifice of Jesus' life, and we are instructed to remember and give thanks.

Food for Thought

1. Each verse of the Psalm emphasizes a different part of the refrain, "Our blessing-cup is a communion with the Blood of Christ." Which verse stands out to you the most, and how has it's meaning changed or been intensified for you?

2. Does this change how you see what God is doing with Jesus at this moment in the story? If so, how?

Second Reading

1 Corinthians 11:23-26

The second reading of the Mass reminds us that the Last Supper was a Passover or Seder meal. The bread that Jesus broke was the unleavened bread of the Seder meal that reminded the Jewish people of the speed of their deliverance. We have already learned about the cups of wine that are part of the meal. It is here, however, that Jesus takes the traditions of the Passover and changes them drastically. The unleavened bread that reminds them of their deliverance from slavery will now be the body that is being sacrificed to deliver them from the slavery of sin. The cup that they will drink is now the cup of the blood of the sacrificial victim, given for their redemption. The body and the blood of the Lamb had never been associated with these items before.

The Jewish people had been told to celebrate the Passover every year to remember that God had delivered them. Jesus tells us the same: "Do this in memory of me." In the same way that the Passover was a sacrifice of communion, this remembrance requires that we participate by eating and drinking the body and blood of the victim in the transformed bread and wine.

■ *1 Corinthians 11:23-26*

> *Brothers and sisters: I received from the Lord what I also handed on to you, that the Lord Jesus, on the night he was handed over, took bread, and after he had given thanks, broke it and said, "This is my body that is for you. Do this in remembrance of me." In the same way also the cup, after supper, saying, "This cup is the new covenant in my blood. Do this, as often as you drink it, in remembrance of me." For as often as you eat this bread and drink the cup, you proclaim the death of the Lord until he comes.*

If we are Catholic, none of these mechanics is too surprising. After all, we've been receiving communion for a long time, and the items offered on the altar are bread and wine. We don't see the disconnect that is significant here. In the eyes of Jesus' disciples, however, taking the bread and wine of the Passover meal and giving them meaning in the coming sacrifice was incredibly odd.

As Jesus takes the bread and the cup, the sacrificial lamb is still on the table. If Jesus is making it clear that He is the Lamb of God, why does He not pick up the lamb and say, "This is my body"? Doesn't that seem to be the most logical thing to do? If Jesus intended to leave us a symbol, the lamb would be the most appropriate item on the table. Instead, Jesus tells us that the bread and the wine are the way that we will participate in this sacrifice of communion. We must consume the victim of the sacrifice, and Jesus is showing us how we are to do it.

Jesus hinted at this idea earlier in His ministry when He said,

> "I am the bread of life. Your ancestors ate the manna in the desert, but they died; this is the bread that comes down from heaven so that one may eat it and not die. I am the living bread that came down from heaven; whoever eats this bread will live forever; and the bread that I will give is my flesh for the life of the world." [1]

This statement was incredibly difficult for people to take as Jesus said it, and many people stopped following Jesus because of it. Rather than explain that He was speaking symbolically, Jesus dug in his heels and asked His apostles if they also wanted to leave, offering no additional explanation in John 6:66-68. [2]

We know that Jesus is the Lamb of God. In the readings from today, we have seen the role of the sacrificial lamb of the Passover, and how Jesus is the fulfillment of that lamb. He has taken this symbol of the Old Testament and fulfilled it with something more. Every one of the symbols that is fulfilled in Jesus is made into something more. The baptism of John the Baptist has been transformed from a ritual cleansing to a point of rebirth in Christ. The role of the High Priest of

---

[1] JOHN 6:48-51

[2] TEXT CAN BE FOUND IN APPENDIX B

Israel, a sinful person who can only enter into the Holy of Holies once a year after being purified, is transformed to the priesthood of the Son of God, who is sinless and has direct access to the throne of God. The Passover lamb of deliverance from slavery and death is now the Lamb who delivers us from slavery to sin and from eternal death.

The bread and the cup of the Passover meal were already symbolic of deliverance. They reminded the Israelites how God had saved them from slavery and death. Why would this be the one symbol from the Old Testament that is transformed into just another symbol rather than something greater? Why would Jesus leave us with something that is less miraculous than the manna He refers to in the Gospel of John? The truth is that He didn't. The bread and the wine are fulfilled here and turned into something greater. No longer symbol, they will truly become for us the Body and Blood of our Lord, Jesus Christ.

Food for Thought

1. God commanded the Jewish people to celebrate the Passover every year in remembrance of their deliverance. Jesus commanded us to "Do this in memory of me." Why would this be important? Was it for God's benefit or for ours?

2. How does the understanding that the sacrifice of Jesus is a sacrifice of communion change your desire to receive the Eucharist?

Gospel

John 13:1-15

In the Gospel for this Mass, we enter into the Upper Room and witness an incredible moment. Jesus stops eating and starts to wash the feet of the disciples. We have no similar situation today that can portray the shock of this scene. Washing the feet of guests was a role given to the lowest of servants, and here is the Messiah, the King that they have waited for, abdicating His role of authority and cleaning their feet.

Today, we see this type of behavior as admirable. Someone with an immense amount of power who serves those less fortunate is applauded for their actions. In Jesus' time, this was completely unthinkable. If you were truly a follower of Jesus, you would protect Him from the consequences of doing something so inappropriate and radical by making Him stop. Clearly, you would never allow Him to wash your own feet.

> *Here he was about to wash my feet, and I could only look on in horror, desperately thinking as Peter did, "Please don't wash my feet."*

Even so, we can have moments when we get a glimpse of what the disciples were feeling. Several years ago, at a retreat, I sat in my chair, realizing that I was about to have my feet washed by my parish priest, and I understood this reading like I never had before. This older gentleman had been instrumental in my husband's coming to faith. He had taken on my husband's questions with gentleness and wisdom, encouraging his explorations and challenges, and guiding him to discover and wrestle with God's truth until my husband was able to claim it for himself. Our lives were completely changed, and I owed much of it to this man. Here he was on his knees about to wash my feet, and I could only look on in horror, desperately thinking as Peter did, "Please don't wash my feet." I owed him so much. The roles should have been completely reversed, and it was all I could do not to pick up this priest and trade places with him.

■ *John 13:1-15*

Before the feast of Passover, Jesus knew that his hour had come to pass from this world to the Father. He loved his own in the world and he loved them to the end. The devil had already induced Judas, son of Simon the Iscariot, to hand him over. So, during supper, fully aware that the Father had put everything into his power and that he had come from God and was returning to God, he rose from supper and took off his outer garments. He took a towel and tied it around his waist. Then he poured water into a basin and began to wash the disciples' feet and dry them with the towel around his waist. He came to Simon Peter, who said to him, "Master, are you going to wash my feet?" Jesus answered and said to him, "What I am doing, you do not understand now, but you will understand later." Peter said to him, "You will never wash my feet." Jesus answered him, "Unless I wash you, you will have no inheritance with me." Simon Peter said to him, "Master, then not only my feet, but my hands and head as well." Jesus said to him, "whoever has bathed has no need except to have his feet washed, for he is clean all over; so you are clean, but not all." For he knew who would betray him; for this reason, he said, "Not all of you are clean."

So when he had washed their feet and put his garments back on and reclined at table again, he said to them, "Do you realize what I have done for you? You call me 'teacher' and 'master,' and rightly so, for indeed I am. If I, therefore, the master and teacher, have washed your feet, you ought to wash one another's feet. I have given you a model to follow, so that as I have done for you, you should also do."

This moment in the Passover meal is here to show all of us that our goal as followers of Christ is never to be about power or having a place at the head of the table. We are called to be of service to all those who are given to us. Our faith is demonstrated in the love that we have for each other. The Gospel shows us that no one is so lowly that he/she are not worthy to have their feet washed by our Lord. No one is so lowly that they cannot be loved by God and by each one of us. If any of us think that we are above this sort of thing, then we are gravely mistaken.

As we celebrate Holy Thursday each year, people from the community are asked to come and have their feet washed. Different churches will do this in different ways, but the tradition is to have 12 people representing the 12 apostles. We take part in the Last Supper just as the apostles did. It is not comfortable for us to have someone else wash our feet. It was not comfortable for the apostles to have Jesus acting in such a subservient way. Even so, we are to remember and follow the model that we have been given.

Food for Thought

1. How would you react if you were chosen as one of the twelve people to have their feet washed?

2. How would you react if you were to wash the feet of someone who could not repay your service, say a homeless person or someone with a severe mental illness?

3. How have you "washed" the feet of those around you recently? Is there someone that you are called to serve right now? How can you do that?

Liturgy of the Eucharist

From here, the Mass looks much as it does every week, but hopefully we have a renewed understanding of what we are doing. We reenact the very meal we have just read about. In the Eucharist, we participate in the New Passover that we have been commanded to observe. We receive the body and the blood of the Lamb of God, and consume them as a part of this sacrifice of communion.

There is much to explore in the standard practice of the Mass, but that would be and has been the topic for an entire book in itself. For now, I will encourage you to allow your experience of this part of the liturgy to be enhanced by the understanding you have gained in this chapter. We have been invited to the table. Blessed are we who are called to the supper of the Lamb.

> **PRESENTATION OF THE HOLY OILS**
>
> At some point in the Mass, the Holy Oils are presented to the parish. Some will have them presented at the beginning of the Mass; others will present them with the gifts as we begin the Liturgy of the Eucharist. These are the oils that will be used throughout the year in the celebration of the sacraments. They are blessed and distributed to all churches in the diocese on Holy Thursday morning.
>
> The Oil of the Sick will be used for the Anointing of the Sick.
>
> The Oil of the Catechumens will be used to anoint those preparing for baptism.
>
> Holy Chrism will be used to anoint infants after baptism, those who are confirmed, bishops and priests at their ordination, and altars and churches as they are dedicated.

> *We know that another way will not be given. The wheels have been set in motion, and in the end, Jesus willingly enters into the will of His Father*

Adoration

After the Passover meal, Jesus leaves with his disciples and goes to the Garden of Gethsemane. He takes Peter, James, and John with him as He goes to pray, leaving them a short distance away and asking them to keep watch.

Jesus is in agony as He asks God to take this cup away from Him. This is the Passover cup of redemption and salvation that has been offered just hours before. This will not be easy, and Jesus asks if there is any other way. We know that another way will not be given. The wheels have been set in motion, and in the end, Jesus willingly enters into the will of His Father.

Jesus returns to Peter, James, and John throughout His prayer, and the three apostles have fallen asleep each and every time. They have no idea what is coming, and they cannot see that Jesus has a reason to be frightened or need consolation. Jesus chastises Peter saying, "So you could not keep watch with me for one hour?" (Matthew 26:40)

In the same way, we leave our Communion Feast and go to the Garden with Jesus. The Hosts are placed in an appropriate container and processed out of the church to a location where they will be placed in an open tabernacle for adoration. After a short time, the tabernacle will be closed, and we are invited to stay with Jesus and pray. Hopefully, we will do better than Peter, James, and John. If we have allowed ourselves to be immersed in the celebration of this week, this garden can be a powerful moment as we become a part of the story.

At some point before midnight, the Blessed Sacrament will be removed. Just as Jesus was arrested and taken from His disciples, He is removed from the Tabernacle and our church is made bare. We will not participate in the new Passover again until the Resurrection.

Every year, my family and I enter into the garden and pray for a while after the main service has ended. Sitting with Jesus in His agony is a powerful and emotional moment for all of us. However, this year for the first time, I came back at the end to spend time with Jesus before He left the garden. It was a very different moment from the beginning.

At the beginning, Jesus is begging God to take this cup of suffering away. There is fear, sadness, and loss filling the moment. He asks three times, "Please take this cup from me." Three times, the answer is "No."

In the end, Jesus answers, "Thy will be done." He knows that God's will is for this sacrifice to be seen through to the very end. It is at this moment that Jesus stands up and leaves the garden in complete control and peace. He could run. He could hide. Instead, Jesus walks to the garden where his arrest is imminent. On the way, he approaches Peter, James, and John, who are sleeping under the tree, and says, "Get up, let us go. Look, my betrayer is at hand."

Being present at the end of this time of adoration, I could see the strength of Jesus as He leaves the garden. From here on out, He is in complete control. This cup will not pass. He will make sure of it. I fell to my knees in awe.

> **IMITATION**
>
> When my children were old enough to understand, I explained to them the meaning and story behind each of the things we did in the Holy Thursday Mass. As we entered into the room set aside for adoration on this night, I reminded them that we were going to the "garden" with Jesus just like the disciples did. My daughter looked at me quizzically and asked, "But, Mommy, we aren't going to sleep are we?" From the mouths of babes...

Food for Thought

1. Whether or not you have participated in Adoration before, how will this moment of prayer be different for you?

2. If Jesus wanted Peter, James, and John to stay awake and pray with Him in His hour of need, what does that tell us about the power of a community of prayer?

Mass Moments

There are many events in the Holy Thursday service. Look over this chapter and think about the things you want to look for, remember, or appreciate as you attend Mass on Holy Thursday. Write them down on the pages in the back.

CHAPTER 3

Good Friday Part 1: Walking the Road to the Cross

There is something within us that desires a physical location to help us remember someone or something significant. We have preserved or reconstructed Abraham Lincoln's birthplace, Thomas Jefferson's home - Monticello, the balcony where Martin Luther King, Jr. was shot, and even Graceland. There is a museum and memorial at the location of the World Trade Center towers that were destroyed on 9/11. Walking through the places where people lived their lives or where a major event occurred helps us to connect with them in a significant and personal way.

We move away from the joy of Palm Sunday, and the light of Holy Thursday. We come to a very dark place, but one that is filled with hidden promises.

How meaningful it must have been for the followers of Jesus to stand in the places that were significant in His life. It's no surprise, then, that it wasn't long before pilgrims started retracing Jesus' steps as He approached the cross. There is evidence that this tradition was in practice as early as the fourth century, with people visiting several sites in Jerusalem. Eventually, the tradition was made available to those who could not travel to Jerusalem as Franciscan monks erected shrines to commemorate the stops on the Via Dolorosa, or Way of Sorrows. By the 1800s, the Stations of the Cross developed into the form that we use today with fourteen stations depicting Jesus' journey from the sentence of death to burial in the tomb. An optional fifteenth station can also be added to include the Resurrection, but we will leave that out here.

The Stations of the Cross are traditionally celebrated during the Lenten season, and during Holy Week, the Stations of the Cross are celebrated in a special way – usually at noon and three o'clock on Good Friday – to commemorate the hour Jesus was placed on the cross, and the hour that He died. In this chapter, we will proceed differently from the others. Each station will consist of the topic, a related scripture, and a reflection. Sit for a moment with each station, meditating on the reality of what was done on the way to the cross. As we are doing in the rest of the Masses of Holy Week, allow yourself to enter into this story. See Jesus looking at you as He walks the Way of the Cross. Be a part of the crowd as you watch Him pass by, and look upon Him as He hangs on the cross. As we begin the events of Good Friday, we move away from the joy of Palm Sunday, with palms and songs of praise, and the light of Holy Thursday, with the joy of the gift of the Eucharist. We come to a very dark place, but one that is filled with hidden promises. Easter is coming, but for now, the price for our sin must be paid. Let us enter in.

The First Station:
Jesus is Condemned to Death

■ *Matthew 27:22-26*

> *Pilate said to them, "Then what shall I do with Jesus called Messiah?" They all said, "Let him be crucified!" But he said, "Why? What evil has he done?" They only shouted the louder, "Let him be crucified!" When Pilate saw that he was not succeeding at all, but that a riot was breaking out instead, he took water and washed his hands in the sight of the crowd, saying, "I am innocent of this man's blood. Look to it yourselves." And the whole people said in reply, "His blood be upon us and upon our children." Then he released Barabbas to them, but after he had Jesus scourged, he handed him over to be crucified.*

When Pilate is interrogating Jesus in the Gospel of John, he tells Jesus that he has the power to release Him or to crucify Him. Jesus answers, "You would have no power over me if it had not been given to you from above." (John 19:11a) When we look at the passage above, we can clearly see that, although Pilate was in a position of power over the Jews, he was powerless to stop the events leading to Jesus' death. Pilate saw the truth. Jesus was an innocent man, and there was no justification for condemning Him to death.

He tries to convince the crowds, declaring that he could find no wrongdoing, and even asking what Jesus had done to deserve such an outcry. Finally, he offers to free a prisoner, as he had traditionally done in honor of the Passover that they were about to celebrate. He offers two choices, thinking that surely this would help the crowds to see the lunacy of their demands. On the one hand is Jesus, this prophet who supposedly claims to be king of the Jews. On the other hand is Barabbas, a murderer who is responsible for rebellion and uprisings.[1] The choice should be simple.

---

[1] IT IS INTERESTING HERE TO NOTE THAT THE NAME BARABBAS MEANS "SON OF THE FATHER." THE CHOICE GIVEN TO THE CROWDS WAS BETWEEN A SON OF A FATHER, AND THE SON OF THE FATHER. IT'S CLOSE, BUT NOT NEARLY THE SAME.

It *is* simple. The crowds call for Barabbas, and the power that Pilate thought he had to release or crucify Jesus is clearly shown to be an illusion.

All power comes from God, whether we see it or not. Our part is to act in it or not. To be grateful for it or not. To cooperate with it or not.

Food for Thought

We think that we have power and control over our lives. Have you had a moment when you realized that wasn't true? How have you seen God's control in your life recently?

The Second Station: Jesus Carries His Cross

- *John 19:16b-17*

    So they took Jesus, and carrying the cross himself, he went out to what is called the Place of the Skull, in Hebrew, Golgotha.

At this point in the story, there is an interesting parallel that comes from the Old Testament. Abraham waits many years to have a son, and he finally receives his promised heir in the birth of Isaac. In Genesis 22:1-13, Abraham is told in a vision to take his son, now much older, to a place three days away and offer him as a sacrifice to God. As they arrive at the mountain, Isaac unknowingly carries the wood for his own sacrifice. He looks around and asks his father about the sheep that they are to sacrifice, since he sees none in the vicinity. Abraham answers, "God himself will provide the sheep." We know the rest of the story. Isaac is saved at the last minute by an angel stopping the hand of Abraham as he starts to sacrifice his son. This will not be required of him, and a ram, caught in a thicket by the horns, is offered in Isaac's place.

In our Gospel scene, as Jesus carries His own cross, the wood needed for his sacrifice, we are reminded of Abraham's sacrifice. In Abraham's case, God did not require the life of his only, beloved son. Knowing that he would offer it was enough. We, on the other hand, demands that the sacrifice be completed. It is not enough to know that God would offer His only, beloved Son, we need to see it through. The lamb has been provided, and His head was surrounded by a crown of thorns, just as the lamb was provided to Abraham and Isaac with its head tangled in the thorns of a thicket. The story of Isaac is not one of a demanding and unreasonable God, but a peek into the plans in the far distant future of a demanding and unreasonable people, and a God who loves them enough to give them what they need.

Food for Thought

Abraham had faith that God would provide what was needed at the time that it was needed. When has God provided for you at just the right time?

The Third Station: Jesus Falls for the First Time

- *Isaiah 53:4-6*

> *Yet it was our pain that he bore,*
>   *our sufferings he endured.*
> *We thought of him as stricken,*
>   *struck down by God and afflicted,*
> *But he was pierced for our sins,*
>   *crushed for our iniquity.*
> *He bore the punishment that makes us whole,*
>   *by his wounds we were healed.*
> *We had all gone astray like sheep,*
>   *all following our own way;*
> *But the LORD laid upon him*
>   *the guilt of us all.*

At this point in the story, Jesus has been scourged in the hopes of satisfying the bloodlust of the crowds. Scourging was not a minor beating, but a severe form of punishment. The whip was made of several straps fastened to a handle and could include pieces of metal or bone to inflict more damage with each stroke. After such a beating, the pain of a cross placed on the wounds inflicted by the whip must have been immense. Falling down was not surprising. It's the getting back up that was unbelievable.

However, staying down was not an option. As long as Jesus had the strength, He would continue on.

As a parent, I understand this on a very small level. Many years ago, my 7-year-old daughter developed an auto-immune disease which, among other symptoms, causes the small blood vessels in your stomach to burst. As you might imagine, open wounds in your stomach are incredibly painful. Since it is a rare disease, it took us a while to get a diagnosis and proper treatment. As her mother, I was by her side helping her deal with the pain, going to doctor after doctor, going in and out of the hospital, and searching for an answer to what was happening to her body. At the same time, I was in the early stages of pregnancy with my fourth child. The exhaustion that comes with that stage is immense. There were times I could hardly stand on my feet. But every time she suffered, I pushed through, and pushed off sleep for another time. There was no way I would leave her alone in this. Ever.

If there was something I could do that would take away suffering for my children, I would do it in a heartbeat. No matter how hard it was, if I knew that my sacrifice would alleviate the suffering of my child, I would get up every time I stumbled. As long as I had an ounce of strength left in my body, I would struggle to my feet and persevere. Most of us don't have the opportunity to do such a thing, but here, Jesus did. He knew without doubt that this would change the world forever, and He got back up.

Food for Thought

Have you had a time when you struggled to help someone? What gave you the strength to continue on? How does this help you appreciate Jesus' struggle while carrying the cross?

The Fourth Station: Jesus Meets His Mother

- *John 19:25-27*

   Standing by the cross of Jesus were his mother and his mother's sister, Mary the wife of Clopas, and Mary of Magdala. When Jesus saw his mother and the disciple there whom he loved, he said to his mother, "Woman, behold, your son." Then he said to the disciple, "Behold, your mother." And from that hour the disciple took her into his home.

On Palm Sunday, we saw Jesus proclaim, "My God, My God, why have you abandoned me?" as He hung on the cross. I wonder, as we come to the place where Mary meets Jesus on the way to His death, if she ever thought the same.

In the movie The Passion of the Christ, Mary is there from the beginning to the end. She watches from the courtyard as Pilate condemns her Son. She sees from the sidelines as He is beaten and returned to His cell. She struggles to follow along the road as He carries His cross, and she sits at His feet as He dies. We don't hear if she fought or if she struggled in the Bible; we only hear that she is there. I wonder – did she doubt, did she question, or did none of it matter, because she was going to be there for Jesus, even if the only thing she could do was to be present?

Many of us have had the experience of helping a sick friend, or maybe even walking the journey with a friend who is dying. As my cousin's young son was dying of a rare, genetic disorder, there was nothing anyone could do. Yet there were so many things that were done for this family. Money was raised to pay medical bills. Donations gave them memorable experiences to give moments of joy within the trial of the illness. People came to visit and spend time in laughter, tears, and anger, sharing in the emotions that swirled about this time of waiting.

These are the times that we can do no more than Mary did. We can't take away the pain, we can't take away the consequences, but we can be present with a fierceness that won't allow even death to stop us. We can be present and offer comfort with our love when there is nothing else we can give. Never underestimate the power in that offering.

Food for Thought

Describe a time that you have been present for someone in his/her suffering. What comfort did you give?

The Fifth Station: Simone of Cyrene Helps Carry the Cross

- *Mark 15:21*

    They pressed into service a passer-by, Simon, a Cyrenian, who was coming in from the country, the father of Alexander and Rufus, to carry his cross.

When we are given crosses to bear, they can be small or they can be quite large. It can be hard to handle when we try to carry them on our own. In this station, we are given witness to the power of our community. This Simon wasn't some random stranger. Mark reminds his readers that this was Simon, the father of Alexander and Rufus. Everyone must have known who that was. He was a member of their community and had an important part to play in our salvation, whether he wanted to or not. If Jesus could not carry His cross alone, how can we ever expect to carry ours without help?

We know that Jesus will help us carry our burdens, but in this moment, we also see that we are given to each other. We will never be left alone in our suffering. We may be pressed into service to help others in bearing their crosses. Someone may be pressed into service to assist us. We are each called to help in Jesus' work of salvation. It is a gift that all of us should be ready to give and be able to receive.

Food for Thought

Name someone who has helped you carry a cross.
Thank God for that person here.

The Sixth Station: Veronica Wipes the Face of Jesus

- *Matthew 25:34-36, 40*

> "Then the king will say to those on his right, 'Come, you who are blessed by my Father. Inherit the kingdom prepared for you from the foundation of the world. For I was hungry and you gave me food, I was thirsty and you gave me drink, a stranger and you welcomed me, naked and you clothed me, ill and you cared for me, in prison and you visited me.' And the king will say to them in reply, 'Amen, I say to you, whatever you did for one of these least brothers of mine, you did for me.'"

This is a traditional station that is not mentioned in the Gospel accounts. Veronica approaches Jesus through the guards and the soldiers, risking punishment in order to offer Jesus comfort as He struggles on the road to Calvary. She takes a cloth, wipes His face, and is left with an impression of Jesus' face on the cloth. Like we see in the Fourth and Fifth Stations, there is blessing in giving small comforts along the way of suffering.

It is hard for many of us to be in the presence of suffering and death. Most of us have no idea what to do or what to say, so we avoid the situation altogether. May these stations remind us that it doesn't matter what we do, it matters that we love. It doesn't matter whether our comfort comes in the form of just being present, actually helping to carry the burden, or wiping the sweat and blood from a brow. When we do that, we are left with the face of Jesus in our hands, knowing that we have served Him well.

Food for Thought

St. Teresa of Calcutta (Mother Teresa) talked about serving Jesus in the "distressing disguise of the poor." What disguise is Jesus wearing near you right now, and how are you serving Him?

The Seventh Station: Jesus Falls the Second Time

- *Isaiah 53:7-8*

> *Though harshly treated, he submitted*
> *and did not open his mouth;*
> *Like a lamb led to slaughter*
> *or a sheep silent before the shearers,*
> *he did not open his mouth.*
> *Seized and condemned, he was taken away.*
> *Who would have thought any more of his destiny?*
> *For he was cut off from the land of the living,*
> *struck for the sins of his people.*

Jesus falls again. He is weak, and even with help, he cannot continue and falls under the weight of the cross. Being 2,000 years from the story, it is easy to make it just that–a story. Even more, we reduce it to an almost cliché phrase, "Jesus died for our sins." The clean, generally well-muscled Jesus that hangs in our churches is less bloody than most children who have fallen on a sidewalk. There might be a little drop of blood on the forehead from a thorn prick, and occasionally there is another drop from the wound on Jesus' side, but overall, He looks pretty good.

Entering into this moment, we start to see that this is much more than a simple sacrifice. This was brutal, and not neat and clean at all. This isn't a story. This is personal.

Watch as Jesus stumbles under the weight of the cross. Look as He struggles to continue with a strength that seems like it cannot possibly last. Know that this was done for you. Know that every sin you have ever done and every sin you will ever do is placed upon that cross, and He will never lay it down, no matter how brutal or ugly it gets. And it's all for you.

Food for Thought

Has Jesus' sacrifice ever felt personal to you? Why or why not?

The Eighth Station: Jesus Meets the Women of Jerusalem

- *Luke 23: 27-28*

    A large crowd of people followed Jesus, including many women who mourned and lamented him. Jesus turned to them and said, "Daughters of Jerusalem, do not weep for me; weep instead for yourselves and for your children."

A friend of mine asked me how I was as we met in the middle of our church parking lot one afternoon. Since I was in the middle of a really bad few days, I spilled all of my frustrations and disappointments right into her lap. Of course, she comforted me, gave me advice, and helped set my perspective back on the right track. As she finished comforting me, I was mortified that I had dared to put all of this upon this woman who was dying of cancer. To the contrary, my friend assured me that this was a role that gave her life and joy. Her suffering would never be enough that she would not be happy to help others in their moments of need.

In this station, Jesus has fallen twice, hardly has the strength to go on, and yet He ministers to the women who mourn for Him as He goes to a brutal death. It is amazing that He is able to focus on anything other than what is happening to Him. Instead, Jesus makes it clear that His situation is not as bad as what is coming. He finishes the statement to the women saying, "for if these things are done when the wood is green, what will happen when it is dry?" (Luke 23: 31) The problem here is not that Jesus is being crucified and that the world has turned its back on Him. Instead, the problem is that the world is willing to destroy the gift that God has given them. They will not accept the truth that is laid before them and cling instead to the truth that allows them to continue living as they would like.

We are given this choice every day. Do we hold onto our own truth, or do we live in God's truth? Do we accept the difficult task of recognizing where we fall short and allow ourselves to be corrected, or do we dismiss these moments as unimportant? The way we act in times when things are easy will be magnified when times are hard. Let us never forget that.

Food for Thought

What truth is Jesus trying to show you lately? Are you listening or resisting?

The Ninth Station: Jesus Falls a Third Time

- *Psalm 37:23-24*

    *The valiant one whose steps are guided by the LORD,
       who will delight in his way,
    May stumble, but he will never fall,
       for the LORD holds his hand.*

When Jesus falls this third time, He is probably within sight of the hill where He is to die. As Jesus continues to stumble with His cross, He knows what He has to do, and He is willing to do it, but He is weak and just can't go one more step. Then He looks up at the people He loves, looks at the reason He is on this path, and stands up again. It's unfathomable. He has just enough strength to finish the journey and lay down His life for us.

If Jesus can struggle with His cross, it is okay that we do, too. We stop, we are in pain, and we want to quit. Then we are given strength we didn't know we had, and we continue on. We will fall, and sometimes we will feel that it is all we do as we fall a second, third, and even fourth time. It is okay. Jesus is right there with us, giving us the strength to get back up and continue on.

Food for Thought

I heard a story once about a newborn giraffe from Gary Richmond's *A View from the Zoo*. The little one struggled to his feet, stood there on wobbly legs, and after a short while, his mother knocked him over. Once more, he shakily got to his feet, only to be knocked down again. Each time, he was a little more confident and steady. Although it seems cruel to the outside observer, the act actually has a significant purpose. The point of the mother was not to knock him over, but to help him remember how to get back up.

Can you look back at times when you have fallen and see where Jesus has helped you stand on your feet? How can that help you when you struggle in the future?

The Tenth Station: Jesus is Stripped of His Clothes

- *John 19: 23-24*

    When the soldiers had crucified Jesus, they took his clothes and divided them into four shares, a share for each soldier. They also took his tunic, but the tunic was seamless, woven in one piece from the top down. So they said to one another, "Let us not tear it, but cast lots for it to see whose it will be," in order that the passage of scripture might be fulfilled [that says]:

    > *"They divided my garments among them,*
    > *and for my vesture they cast lots."*

You may recognize the scripture about dividing the garments from Psalm 22 on Palm Sunday. This verse is being played out right here in this Station. Jesus is stripped of His clothing, and the guards each take a piece for themselves. It's barbaric and cruel. It is interesting to note here that the tunic was not divided or torn.

In the Gospel of John, the mention of the tunic is significant because the priests in the Temple wore seamless garments. This garment set them apart and marked them as priests of God. The work that the priests of Jerusalem were doing this day as Jesus hung from the cross was the same as the work Jesus was doing on the cross. The Passover lambs were being slaughtered, offered for the deliverance of the people, offered by the priests who had been given the power and the authority to do so. The priests in the temple were covered in the blood of the symbolic lambs. The priest on the cross was covered in the blood of the last sacrifice required by God, the true Lamb, given for the forgiveness of all sins for all time.

Food for Thought

Jesus fulfills many roles: priest, victim, temple, food, Son, prophet, law, Savior, etc. What role or position does Jesus play in your life right now?

The Eleventh Station: Jesus is Nailed to the Cross

- *Luke 23:33-34a*

    When they came to the place called the Skull, they crucified him and the criminals there, one on his right, the other on his left. [Then Jesus said, "Father, forgive them, they know not what they do."]

As Jesus hangs from the cross, He has every reason to call down punishment and judgment on the people who place Him there and on the people who come by to look and jeer at Him. He has the power to condemn any of them, from Judas to Pilate to Peter, but He refuses to do so. Instead, He asks for them to be forgiven. He asks for each and every one of them. Where does He find the strength to forgive them?

He can do this because He can see the other side of the story. He can see them through the eyes of their Creator. He can see that this sacrifice must be made, and if they had any idea what they were doing, it would be stopped. He can see that they can't see, because their eyes have been clouded by sin, pride, and fear. He can see that they can't see, because their eyes are searching for someone powerful and strong to lead them, not someone meek and servile to guide them. He can see that they are lost and need a shepherd to lead them home, and He wants to lead them home more than anything. "Forgive them, Lord. They know not what they do." Forgive us, Lord, when we don't know what we do.

Food for Thought

Is there someone you need to forgive? Does it help if you can see the other side of their story?

The Twelfth Station: Jesus Dies on the Cross

- *Luke 23: 44-46*

    It was now about noon and darkness came over the whole land until three in the afternoon because of an eclipse of the sun. Then the veil of the temple was torn down the middle. Jesus cried out in a loud voice, "Father, into your hands I commend my spirit"; and when he had said this he breathed his last.

It is finished.

As we walk this road with Jesus, the entire thing is not very long – less than twenty-four hours actually. Less than twenty-four hours of anticipation, terror, pain, suffering, and death. Most other days, twenty-four hours pass in the blink of an eye, but this day, twenty-four hours is long, arduous, and cruel. As I watched *The Passion of the Christ*, I remember desperately wanting the pain and suffering to stop.

At some point, death is a blessing. It is a blessing that the suffering is over, and the victim has been released from the agony of the process. We sit at this moment, and we gaze upon Jesus, who has given us everything He had to give. Receive it. Hold this gift tenderly in your heart. Give thanks that you have Someone who loves you this much.

Food for Thought

Sit with this gift for a moment. Write down your thoughts here.

The Thirteenth Station: The Body of Jesus is Taken Down from the Cross

■ *John 19: 32-34, 38*

So the soldiers came and broke the legs of the first and then of the other one who was crucified with Jesus. But when they came to Jesus and saw that he was already dead, they did not break his legs, but one soldier thrust his lance into his side, and immediately blood and water flowed out.

After this, Joseph of Arimathea, secretly a disciple of Jesus for fear of the Jews, asked Pilate if he could remove the body of Jesus. And Pilate permitted it. So he came and took his body.

The end seems so quiet. No more struggle, no more to be done. Just a little cleanup. The demands of the crowd have been met. Jesus is dead.

Michelangelo's Pieta poignantly shows us the aftermath of the crucifixion as Mary holds the body of her son, Jesus. Now the ones who love Him can tend to what is left. The people who knew Him best were kept in darkness and allowed to believe and feel the impact of this death.

We know that Jesus' death is not the end. Jesus has been lifted up and given over, but the rest of the story must wait. For now, He must be taken down and buried.

Food for Thought

Waiting can be so hard, especially if things look hopeless. What helps you to continue when something you want or need isn't coming right away?

The Fourteenth Station: Jesus is Laid in the Tomb

- *John 19:39-42*

    Nicodemus, the one who had first come to him at night, also came bringing a mixture of myrrh and aloes weighing about one hundred pounds. They took the body of Jesus and bound it with burial cloths along with the spices, according to the Jewish burial custom. Now in the place where he had been crucified there was a garden, and in the garden a new tomb, in which no one had yet been buried. So they laid Jesus there because of the Jewish preparation day; for the tomb was close by.

In the beginning there was a Garden. In the beginning there was a tree. In the beginning there was a fall from grace that started everything here in motion. In the end, as Jesus is laid to rest, there is another garden, there is another tree, and the fall is reversed. The cost of sin that began with disobedience is redeemed through an act filled with obedience.

As Jesus is laid in the tomb, all may seem to be lost. This is not a comfortable place for us. It is hard to sit in times of darkness and fear, but we know that God can accomplish His greatest work in the darkest of times. Today as Joseph, Nicodemus and the others return to their homes, we leave here as well. Jesus is hidden from our view, and we will wait.

Food for Thought

As we conclude the Stations of the Cross, what are your thoughts about the events of Jesus' Passion? Has the meaning or story changed for you?

We close these Stations with a prayer that is traditionally said at the beginning of each Station:

"We adore you, O Christ, and we praise you. For by your holy cross, you have redeemed the world."

Mass Moments

While this is not technically a part of the Mass, it is a traditional practice on Good Friday. Look over this chapter and think about the things you want to look for, remember, or appreciate as you participate in the Stations of the Cross. Write them down on the pages in the back.

CHAPTER 4

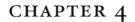

Good Friday Part 2: The Freely Given Sacrifice

We love predictions, don't we? Whether we are predicting the weather, the outcome of a football game, or the biggest trend of the future, we're always trying to get a glimpse into what is coming next. The stock market is notorious for predictions, with analysts trying to tell you that they know what will happen in the next six months, the next year, and the next ten years. Interestingly enough, studies have shown that the predictions of analysts average out to being correct less than 50% of the time.[1] That's worse than the probability of a coin flip. Even predicting the outcome of March Madness is so uncertain that Warren Buffet offered a $1 billion prize for anyone who could correctly predict the winners of all 63 games of the 2016 NCAA men's college basketball tournament. No one won the prize.

Today as we enter into the Good Friday celebration, we will see some predictions or prophesies that came true in astonishing ways. Jesus tried to explain what was coming numerous times throughout His ministry, but no one understood it until after the Resurrection. The New Testament remained hidden in the Old as it was being lived in Jesus. As these events unfolded on that fateful Friday, it had to have been confusing, devastating, and terrifying for those who had yet to understand the predictions. Today we enter into that moment in an up close and personal way with the gift of hindsight. We know how the story ends, so we get to see how the predictions unfold. Let us begin.

---

[1] "GURU GRADES." CXO ADVISORY RSS. CXO ADVISORY GROUP, LLC, N.D. WEB. 08 NOV. 2016.

Preparation

This is the second day of the Triduum, the three day Mass. When we left last night, Jesus was taken from the garden. As we enter today, the altar has been stripped, there are no candles, no flowers, and no holy water. The tabernacle is open and empty, and the Sanctuary lamp, a candle indicating the presence of Jesus in the tabernacle, has been removed. Today Jesus is taken from our view. It is desolate, and it is disturbing, but holy work is being done.

Entry

Today we start in silence. There is no entrance hymn because we are picking up where we left off last night. The priests enter in red vestments. As we saw on Palm Sunday, this red is a signal to us that a sacrifice is being offered. Blood will be spilled today, and we treasure that blood for the life that is contained within it.

Depending on the size of the church, there may be several priests and deacons celebrating this Mass. As they enter, all of them will approach the altar and prostrate themselves (lay down) in front of it while the congregation kneels. The clergy show in a very physical way the humility and sorrow that we have as we approach the sacrifice of Easter. It's a form of prayer that most of us haven't ever done or even heard of, but in our kneeling and our standing during Mass, we have a glimpse of the power of the physical expression of prayer.

> *The tabernacle is open and empty. Today, Jesus is taken from our view. It is desolate, and it is disturbing, but holy work is being done.*

Laying in front of someone, face down, with arms extended, is an incredibly vulnerable and humbling position. I have never done this as I have prayed in church, but I have had a time in my home when I was very aware of the wonder and awesomeness of God who loves me more than anything I could fathom. Standing in the presence of such love, I could only lay myself in front of Him, offering everything I have and everything that I am. It was an incredible moment of intimacy and grace.

As we stand before Jesus today, we are face-to-face with Him as He hangs from the cross. We know the suffering that He is willing to endure for us, and we know that He will even die for us. We know that *our* sins put Him there. If we truly understand this, how could we do anything but lay in front of Him in gratitude and love, knowing that nothing we could offer would ever be worthy of what Jesus has done?

> *As we stand before Jesus today, we are face-to-face with Him as He hangs from the cross. We know that our sins put Him there. If we truly understand this, how could we do anything by lay in front of Him in gratitude and love?*

Most of us have never had a personal experience of having someone offer his or her life for ours, so it is hard to comprehend what Jesus' sacrifice means when we are 2,000 years away from the event. To help us understand, we will look at Saint Maximillian Kolbe. In the German concentration camp of Auschwitz, ten prisoners were selected from the camp to die in a starvation hut as punishment for the escape of three prisoners. As one man's name was called, he asked for mercy since he was a husband and a father. Fr. Maximillian Kolbe stepped forward and freely offered to take his place. He entered into the hut and ministered to all who had been condemned, filling the room with prayer, singing, joy, and peace. Finally, after all the others had died, the guards injected him with carbolic acid to empty the bunker since he was taking so long to die.

Can you imagine standing before Father Kolbe as he left for the bunker in your place? Imagine knowing day after day for two weeks that he was dying instead of you. What would you say? What would you do if you saw him again? There would be no way you could adequately express your gratitude, and I imagine there would be no way that you could ever feel worthy of such a gift.

None of us is worthy of such a sacrifice. As Paul says, "Indeed, only with difficulty does one die for a just person, though perhaps for a good person one might even find courage to die. But God proves his love for us in that while we were still sinners Christ died for us." (Romans 5:7-8)

As we begin today, we come face to face with Jesus, who is walking to the cross in our place. He is paying the price for any sin we could ever possibly commit. We need only to repent of our sin and accept the offer. When we truly understand this, we fall prostrate, or at the very least, fall to our knees in the presence of the one who so freely offers His life for us.

First Reading

Isaiah 52:13-53:12

Our first reading was written 700 years before Jesus was born. As we saw at the beginning of this chapter, predictions for events happening months or weeks away are rarely more accurate than a coin flip. To predict something 700 years in advance is astounding, yet this prophesy not only tells of the general event, but gives specific details. Note the descriptions in this passage that apply to Jesus and His crucifixion. With so much accuracy, we can trust that the work God is doing in the sacrifice of Jesus brings about the effect that is promised in this reading as well.

- *Isaiah 52:13-53:12*

   See, my servant shall prosper,
      he shall be raised high and greatly exalted.
   Even as many were amazed at him—
      so marred was his look beyond human semblance
      and his appearance beyond that of the sons of man –
   so shall he startle many nations,
      because of him kings shall stand speechless;
   for those who have not been told shall see,
      those who have not heard shall ponder it.

   Who would believe what we have heard?
      To whom has the arm of the LORD been revealed?
   He grew up like a sapling before him,
      like a shoot from the parched earth;
   there was in him no stately bearing to make us look at him,
      nor appearance that would attract us to him.
   He was spurned and avoided by people,
      a man of suffering, accustomed to infirmity,
   one of those from whom people hide their faces,
      spurned, and we held him in no esteem.

Yet it was our infirmities he bore,
 our sufferings that he endured,
while we thought of him as stricken,
 as one smitten by God and afflicted.
But he was pierced for our offenses,
 crushed for our sins;
upon him was the chastisement that makes us whole,
 by his stripes we were healed.
We had all gone astray like sheep,
 each following his own way;
but the LORD laid upon him
 the guilt of us all.

Though he was harshly treated, he submitted
 and opened not his mouth;
like a lamb led to the slaughter
 or a sheep before the shearers,
 he was silent and opened not his mouth.
Oppressed and condemned, he was taken away,
 and who would have thought any more of his destiny?
When he was cut off from the land of the living,
 and smitten for the sin of his people,
a grave was assigned him among the wicked
 and a burial place with evildoers,
though he had done no wrong
 nor spoken any falsehood.
But the LORD was pleased
 to crush him in infirmity.

If he gives his life as an offering for sin,
 he shall see his descendants in a long life,
 and the will of the LORD shall be accomplished through him.

Because of his affliction
 he shall see the light in fullness of days;
through his suffering, my servant shall justify many,
 and their guilt he shall bear.
Therefore I will give him his portion among the great,
 and he shall divide the spoils with the mighty,
because he surrendered himself to death
 and was counted among the wicked;
and he shall take away the sins of many
 and win pardon for their offenses.

This passage was originally written for the Israelites as they were in exile. These descriptions were filling in the picture of the Messiah who would restore their kingdom. Reading this without the context of the role of Jesus would have been very confusing. How could someone who is pierced, cut off from the land of the living, in the grave, and giving his life as an offering for sin see the light in fullness of days, and see his descendants in a long life? How can he divide the spoils with the mighty if he is dead? This passage is obviously not talking about someone who was saved from death, but talking about someone whose death is very effective for bringing about some sort of new life.

Those of us who have the benefit of the rest of the story can see that Jesus was harshly treated, and we have heard how people jeered at Him and believed that God had abandoned Him. He was considered evil, but He had done nothing wrong. We have been told that what we see does not look like what is being done. This is the paradox of the cross. The shame of the world is the glory of God. It's a stumbling block for many, both then and now.

Food for Thought

1. Why do you think it would be important for this passage to be written so long before Jesus was even born?

2. Does it make a difference in your faith or belief? Why or why not?

Responsorial Psalm *Psalm 31: 2, 6, 12-13, 15-16, 17, 25*

This Psalm is another Old Testament reference that paints a picture of what is happening on the hill at Calvary. See if you recognize what is happening on Good Friday in these verses that were written so many years before.

■ *Psalm 31: 2, 6, 12-13, 15-16, 17, 25*

    R. (Luke 23:46) Father, into your hands I commend my spirit.

In you, O LORD, I take refuge;
    let me never be put to shame.
In your justice rescue me.
Into your hands I commend my spirit;
    you will redeem me, O LORD, O faithful God.

    R. Father, into your hands I commend my spirit.

For all my foes I am an object of reproach,
    a laughingstock to my neighbors, and a dread to my friends;
    they who see me abroad flee from me.
I am forgotten like the unremembered dead;
    I am like a dish that is broken.

R. Father, into your hands I commend my spirit.

But my trust is in you, O LORD;
    I say, "You are my God.
Into your hands is my destiny; rescue me
    from the clutches of my enemies and my persecutors."

R. Father, into your hands I commend my spirit.

Let your face shine upon your servant;
    save me in your kindness.
Take courage and be stouthearted,
    all you who hope in the LORD.

R. Father, into your hands I commend my spirit.

You may recognize this refrain. In Luke 23:46, Jesus proclaims, "Father, into your hands I commend my spirit" from the cross, and dies. Just as He did with Psalm 22, Jesus is saying much more in this statement from Psalm 31, and the people watching Him on the cross would understand the reference. Still, this would have seemed ironic. As Jesus refers to a Psalm that claims confidence in God's redemption and rescue from enemies, He dies and His confidence seems to be misplaced. Everything today, as we will see, is backwards. Nothing is as it seems. Evil seems to have won the day, and Jesus appears to be no more than another false hope for those waiting for a Savior.

The scene reminds me of C.S. Lewis' The Lion, the Witch, and the Wardrobe. Aslan the Lion is murdered by the White Witch to pay for the transgression of Edmund, one of the humans in the story. There is a Deep Magic that must be satisfied, and because of it, the White Witch is owed the life of the transgressor. Instead, Aslan, the ruler of the land, offers to give his life as payment for the debt. The price will be paid, and the White Witch's enemy, Aslan, will be vanquished all in one stroke if she accepts his offer. She joyfully and triumphantly accepts the exchange.

However, when he returns to life, Aslan explains, "though the Witch knew the Deep Magic, there is a magic deeper still which she did not know... when a willing victim who had committed no treachery was killed in a traitor's stead, the table would crack and Death itself would start working backward."

In the same way, Jesus' work today pays the price for sin and so much more. Jesus' spirit is given to the Father, and the price of justice is satisfied not just for now, not just for Jesus or the people who are present at the crucifixion, but for all time to come.

Food for Thought

1. If you knew this Psalm, and heard Jesus reference it from the cross, would it have brought you comfort or sorrow if you were one of Jesus' followers?

2. Have you seen or been in a situation that seems on the surface to be a failure, but turns out to be something positive? What happened?

Second Reading

Hebrews 4:14-17, 5:7-9

In order to understand this reading, you have to know about the role of the high priest in Judaism. In the Jewish Temple, there were three distinct areas. There was an outer court where people could gather, an inner court where sacrifices and worship took place, and the center area, called the Holy of Holies. The Holy of Holies was considered the dwelling place of God, and the Ark of the Covenant was kept there.

Only the high priest was ever allowed to enter the Holy of Holies, and only once per year on Yom Kippur, or the Day of Atonement. The purpose was to offer the blood of sacrifice on the mercy seat of the Ark of the Covenant. A goat had to be sacrificed for the people, and its life in the form of its blood was offered as payment for their sins. This offering was done every year because every year, the people sinned. The only person who could make this offering was the high priest, and even then he had to be purified beforehand.

■ *Hebrews 4:14-16; 5:7-9*

Brothers and sisters:

Since we have a great high priest who has passed through the heavens, Jesus, the Son of God, let us hold fast to our confession. For we do not have a high priest who is unable to sympathize with our weaknesses, but one who has similarly been tested in every way, yet without sin. So let us confidently approach the throne of grace to receive mercy and to find grace for timely help.

In the days when Christ was in the flesh, he offered prayers and supplications with loud cries and tears to the one who was able to save him from death, and he was heard because of his reverence. Son though he was, he learned obedience from what he suffered; and when he was made perfect, he became the source of eternal salvation for all who obey him.

The book of Hebrews reminds us that the roles of the high priest and sacrifice have been fulfilled in Jesus. This high priest is not here among us, needing to be purified in order to enter into the presence of God. Jesus is continually in the presence of God, offering Himself for us. Not only that, He knows us. He has lived like us, and He understands and loves us for it.

Shortly in our service today, as Jesus dies, the veil to the Holy of Holies will be torn in half, and the innermost part of the Temple will be opened. We have free access to the mercy seat. The blood of the perfect victim has been offered, and we are invited to enter.

Food for Thought

1. How do you approach God?

2. Do you feel like you can go to God directly? Why or why not?

Gospel

As we enter the Gospel, let me remind you that everything today seems to be backwards. Look for these moments and more as you read:

1. Four hundred soldiers come to arrest one person, Jesus. Jesus is innocent of anything, by the way.
2. As they ask for Jesus, he answers, "I AM," and they fall down in fear rather than Jesus being afraid of them.
3. The high priests bring Jesus to Pontius Pilate and say that He needs to be crucified because He is a criminal even though the charges they bring are false. Who are the ones doing the wrong thing here?
4. Pilate tells the crowd that Jesus is innocent, and they react by demanding His crucifixion.
5. Pilate tells Jesus that he is in control and that he can release Jesus if he wants. When Pilate tries to release Him, what happens? Is Pilate really in control?
6. A judge delivers a verdict to the accused from the judge's bench, dictating who is innocent and may go free, and who is guilty and must be punished. Pilate sits Jesus in the judge's bench and declares Jesus king of the Jews, but the punishment is death. Who is the true judge? If Jesus is the judge, who is guilty? Who is the punishment for?

As we go through the Gospel, look for the moments when truth is told or when things are the opposite of what they seem to be. I will include some of them throughout the reading, but there are many more.

The truth of who Jesus is and what He is doing is so intermingled with the truth of our sin and our separation from God, that it was lost at the time. It's not so different now, even when we know the story. We can get turned around and lost in our sin and see the good being offered as something bad to be avoided. May this Gospel help to open our eyes to the truth.

- *John 18:1-19:42*

    Jesus went out with his disciples across the Kidron valley to where there was a garden, into which he and his disciples entered. Judas his betrayer also knew the place, because Jesus had often met there with his disciples. So Judas got a band of soldiers and guards from the chief priests and the Pharisees and went there with lanterns, torches, and weapons. Jesus, knowing everything that was going to happen to him, went out and said to them, "Whom are you looking for?" They answered him, "Jesus the Nazorean." He said to them, "I AM." Judas his betrayer was also with them. When he said to them, "I AM," they turned away and fell to the ground. So he again asked them, "Whom are you looking for?" They said, "Jesus the Nazorean." Jesus answered, "I told you that I AM. So if you are looking for me, let these men go." This was to fulfill what he had said, "I have not lost any of those you gave me." Then Simon Peter, who had a sword, drew it, struck the high priest's slave, and cut off his right ear. The slave's name was Malchus. Jesus said to Peter, "Put your sword into its scabbard. Shall I not drink the cup that the Father gave me?"

    So the band of soldiers, the tribune, and the Jewish guards seized Jesus, bound him, and brought him to Annas first. He was the father-in-law of Caiaphas, who was high priest that year. It was Caiaphas who had counseled the Jews that it was better that one man should die rather than the people.

Notice the moments when truth is apparent, but misinterpreted:

- The soldiers fall to the ground as Jesus says, "I AM" much like the priests did as they entered tonight.
- "One man should die rather than the people." Caiaphas was referring to the Jewish people dying at the hands of Roman soldiers, but Jesus will fulfill this statement so that all people will have access to eternal life.

Simon Peter and another disciple followed Jesus. Now the other disciple was known to the high priest, and he entered the courtyard of the high priest with Jesus. But Peter stood at the gate outside. So the other disciple, the acquaintance of the high priest, went out and spoke to the gatekeeper and brought Peter in. Then the maid who was the gatekeeper said to Peter, "You are not one of this man's disciples, are you?" He said, "I am not." Now the slaves and the guards were standing around a charcoal fire that they had made, because it was cold, and were warming themselves. Peter was also standing there keeping warm.

The high priest questioned Jesus about his disciples and about his doctrine. Jesus answered him, "I have spoken publicly to the world. I have always taught in a synagogue or in the temple area where all the Jews gather, and in secret I have said nothing. Why ask me? Ask those who heard me what I said to them. They know what I said." When he had said this, one of the temple guards standing there struck Jesus and said, "Is this the way you answer the high priest?" Jesus answered him, "If I have spoken wrongly, testify to the wrong; but if I have spoken rightly, why do you strike me?" Then Annas sent him bound to Caiaphas the high priest.

Now Simon Peter was standing there keeping warm. And they said to him, "You are not one of his disciples, are you?" He denied it and said, "I am not." One of the slaves of the high priest, a relative of the one whose ear Peter had cut off, said, "Didn't I see you in the garden with him?" Again Peter denied it. And immediately the cock crowed.

Notice the moments of contrast between Jesus and the others in the story:

- Jesus identified Himself by saying, "I AM." Peter denies who he is by saying, "I am not," even when the man who watched Peter cut off his cousin's ear recognizes him. Chances are good that this man would remember Peter pretty clearly.
- Jesus said everything during the day in public, and nothing in secret. The religious leaders are trying him at night and in secret.

Then they brought Jesus from Caiaphas to the praetorium. It was morning. And they themselves did not enter the praetorium, in order not to be defiled so that they could eat the Passover. So Pilate came out to them and said, "What charge do you bring against this man?" They answered and said to him, "If he were not a criminal, we would not have handed him over to you." At this, Pilate said to them, "Take him yourselves, and judge him according to your law." The Jews answered him, "We do not have the right to execute anyone," in order that the word of Jesus might be fulfilled that he said indicating the kind of death he would die. So Pilate went back into the praetorium and summoned Jesus and said to him, "Are you the King of the Jews?" Jesus answered, "Do you say this on your own or have others told you about me?" Pilate answered, "I am not a Jew, am I? Your own nation and the chief priests handed you over to me. What have you done?" Jesus answered, "My kingdom does not belong to this world. If my kingdom did belong to this world, my attendants would be fighting to keep me from being handed over to the Jews. But as it is, my kingdom is not here." So Pilate said to him, "Then you are a king?" Jesus answered, "You say I am a king. For this I was born and for this I came into the world, to testify to the truth. Everyone who belongs to the truth listens to my voice." Pilate said to him, "What is truth?"

When he had said this, he again went out to the Jews and said to them, "I find no guilt in him. But you have a custom that I release one prisoner to you at Passover. Do you want me to release to you the King of the Jews?" They cried out again, "Not this one but Barabbas!" Now Barabbas was a revolutionary.

Notice the things that are backwards as Pilate enters the story:

- The leaders refuse to enter a Gentile building because it would make them impure, yet they are asking for the death of an innocent man. Jesus, who is completely pure, is in the praetorium.
- When asked for the charges against Jesus, the leaders proclaim that they wouldn't have brought Him if He hadn't done anything wrong. Pilate then asks Jesus for the charges – "What have you done?"

Then Pilate took Jesus and had him scourged. And the soldiers wove a crown out of thorns and placed it on his head, and clothed him in a purple cloak, and they came to him and said, "Hail, King of the Jews!" And they struck him repeatedly. Once more Pilate went out and said to them, "Look, I am bringing him out to you, so that you may know that I find no guilt in him." So Jesus came out, wearing the crown of thorns and the purple cloak. And he said to them, "Behold, the man!" When the chief priests and the guards saw him they cried out, "Crucify him, crucify him!" Pilate said to them, "Take him yourselves and crucify him. I find no guilt in him." The Jews answered, "We have a law, and according to that law he ought to die, because he made himself the Son of God." Now when Pilate heard these statements, he became even more afraid, and went back into the praetorium and said to Jesus, "Where are you from?" Jesus did not answer him. So Pilate said to him, "Do you not speak to me? Do you not know that I have power to release you, and I have power to crucify you?" Jesus answered him, "You would have no power over me if it had not been given to you from above. For this reason the one who handed me over to you has the greater sin." Consequently, Pilate tried to release him; but the Jews cried out, "If you release him, you are not a Friend of Caesar. Everyone who makes himself a king opposes Caesar."

When Pilate heard these words he brought Jesus out and seated him on the judge's bench in the place called Stone Pavement, in Hebrew, Gabbatha. It was preparation day for Passover and it was about noon. And he said to the Jews, "Behold, your king!" They cried out, "Take him away, take him away! Crucify him!" Pilate said to them, "Shall I crucify your king?" The chief priests answered, "We have no king but Caesar." Then he handed him over to them to be crucified.

Notice how the truth of Jesus is proclaimed, yet distorted in this part of the story:

- He is presented as king with a crown and robe – the crown is of thorns, and the robe is a simple cloak.
- Pilate proclaims, "Behold, your king!" and the chief priests reply, "We have no king but Caesar." They hated the rule of Caesar and were waiting for a Messiah to deliver them from Roman rule. They have fully rejected their true king and claim what they abhor.

So they took Jesus, and, carrying the cross himself, he went out to what is called the Place of the Skull, in Hebrew, Golgotha. There they crucified him, and with him two others, one on either side, with Jesus in the middle. Pilate also had an inscription written and put on the cross. It read, "Jesus the Nazorean, the King of the Jews." Now many of the Jews read this inscription, because the place where Jesus was crucified was near the city; and it was written in Hebrew, Latin, and Greek. So the chief priests of the Jews said to Pilate, "Do not write 'The King of the Jews,' but that he said, 'I am the King of the Jews'." Pilate answered, "What I have written, I have written."

When the soldiers had crucified Jesus, they took his clothes and divided them into four shares, a share for each soldier. They also took his tunic, but the tunic was seamless, woven in one piece it will be, " in order that the passage of Scripture might be fulfilled that says:

>   *They divided my garments among them,*
>   *and for my vesture they cast lots.*

This is what the soldiers did. Standing by the cross of Jesus were his mother and his mother's sister, Mary the wife of Clopas, and Mary of Magdala. When Jesus saw his mother and the disciple there whom he loved he said to his mother, "Woman, behold, your son." Then he said to the disciple, "Behold, your mother." And from that hour the disciple took her into his home.

After this, aware that everything was now finished, in order that the Scripture might be fulfilled, Jesus said, "I thirst." There was a vessel filled with common wine. So they put a sponge soaked in wine on a sprig of hyssop and put it up to his mouth. When Jesus had taken the wine, he said, "It is finished." And bowing his head, he handed over the spirit.

Notice the roles that Jesus fulfills in the moments leading to His death:

- King: "King of the Jews" is written in three languages. This is a King for all people, not just those who speak Hebrew.
- Priest: Jesus' tunic is seamless, like that of a priest of the Temple. It is not torn, and His priesthood is not destroyed with His death.
- Passover Lamb: The wine Jesus drinks is placed on a sprig of hyssop, the same branch used to spread the blood of the Passover lamb on the doorposts. He drinks it as He gives His life for us.

Now since it was preparation day, in order that the bodies might not remain on the cross on the sabbath, for the sabbath day of that week was a solemn one, the Jews asked Pilate that their legs be broken and that they be taken down. So the soldiers came and broke the legs of the first and then of the other one who was crucified with Jesus. But when they came to Jesus and saw that he was already dead, they did not break his legs, but one soldier thrust his lance into his side, and immediately blood and water flowed out. An eyewitness has testified, and his testimony is true; he knows that he is speaking the truth, so that you also may come to believe. For this happened so that the Scripture passage might be fulfilled:

Not a bone of it will be broken.[1]

And again another passage says:

They will look upon him whom they have pierced.[2]

After this, Joseph of Arimathea, secretly a disciple of Jesus for fear of the Jews, asked Pilate if he could remove the body of Jesus. And Pilate permitted it. So he came and took his body. Nicodemus, the one who had first come to him at night, also came bringing a mixture of myrrh and aloes weighing about one hundred pounds. They took the body of Jesus and bound it with burial cloths along with the spices, according to the Jewish burial custom. Now in the place where he had been

---

[1] EXODUS 12:46; NUMBERS 9:12, PSALM 34:21

[2] NUMBERS 21:9; ZECHARIAH 12:10

crucified there was a garden, and in the garden a new tomb, in which no one had yet been buried. So they laid Jesus there because of the Jewish preparation day; for the tomb was close by.

Notice the moments of fulfillment as the Gospel reading draws to a close:

- After Jesus' death, He fulfills the role of Passover Lamb ("Not a bone shall be broken") and of the Messiah ("They shall look upon him whom they have pierced.")
- In the garden, the fall of the first Garden is reversed. Jesus' obedience counters the disobedience of Adam and Eve.

Food for Thought

1. Did you find any other moments of truth or disconnect with the truth? What were they? (More are listed in Appendix C)

2. Why do we resist the truth of God and Jesus' salvation? If it is offered so freely, what could prevent us from accepting it?

3. Have you had a moment when you realized the enormity of what Jesus has done for you? What was it like?

4. Look at the number of times that Pilate proclaims the truth in this Gospel reading. Even though he knows and proclaims the truth, it doesn't change the events that lead to the cross. Is there a time when you have proclaimed the truth, but had to watch as it was ignored or rejected? What did God do with that situation?

> **NUMBERS**
>
> Whenever you see a three in the Bible, it is a significant number. Biblically, it represents the Trinity, holiness, and completion. The number three is present throughout the story and Masses of Holy Week. There are three crosses on the hill, Jesus is dead for three days, and Jesus falls three times, just to name a few. Keep an eye out for them.

Veneration of the Cross

As we continue our Mass, the cross is brought out for us to venerate. "Venerate" is a word that is commonly confused with "worship." While the two actions may look similar, the intention is quite different. To venerate is defined by Merriam-Webster as "to regard with reverential respect or with admiring deference, or to honor (as an icon or relic) with a ritual act of devotion."[1] When we venerate something, we acknowledge its special role and special place in our lives of faith.

The cross on display in front of us is not the cross that held Jesus as He died. We are aware of that. It is a concrete representation that is brought out to help us connect physically to the past. We are a physical people, and having something that we can see and touch allows us to connect more deeply and more meaningfully if we will allow it to do so. We did the same in the Stations of the Cross. Remember this as we start this part of the service.

As the cross is brought out, it can be carried in or it can be placed in front of the people. In the process, it is lifted and uncovered in three stages. We lift the cross and slowly reveal the horrific tool of the sacrifice that has been offered for us. When the cross is fully revealed, we are invited to come and venerate. We are invited to come and touch and remember. We are invited to come close and see what has been done for us. If you allow yourself to enter into the story, it can be an incredibly powerful moment.

Conclusion

We complete this day with a simple, barren communion service. There is no consecration today. Rather, we use the consecrated hosts that were blessed on Holy Thursday. We recite The Lord's Prayer along with a couple of simple blessings, and we receive communion. We cannot celebrate the full Mass today. Jesus is dead, and He is hidden from our sight. At this point, the disciples of Jesus were sad, devastated, confused, terrified, and scattered. Their leader and their Lord has died and is laid in the tomb. It is the Sabbath, and the celebration of the Passover, so there is nothing that can be done until the next day is over.

---

[1] *MERRIAM-WEBSTER.* MERRIAM-WEBSTER, N.D. WEB. 15 NOV. 2016.

We leave in silence, placing ourselves with them as we walk away from this horrific event. How could this have happened? Why would God allow such a thing? Why would Jesus comply so freely? So many questions, so many feelings. If we allow ourselves to be present at this moment, we must leave here with the questions unanswered, as the disciples did, with nothing to do but wait.

GETTING IT RIGHT

When my youngest child was little, she tugged at my sleeve as we prepared to approach the cross for veneration. The poor thing was well aware of the reality of death due to the recent death of a family friend who was about the same age as I was. She was embarrassed and didn't want to cause a scene, but she had no desire to be anywhere near that cross. At the same time, she didn't want to be separated from me when I went forward. As tears filled her eyes, I told her that she didn't have to go. Instead, she could walk with me down the aisle and move to the side as I went forward to the cross.

Afterwards, we went out into the hallway as she struggled with her "overreaction." It was then that I could tell her that she was having the most rational reaction that there could be. Everyone should be reacting as she did. The cross was horrific, it was awful, and it was painful. It was even too hard for Jesus' disciples to bear. Only a couple of them were there with Him as He died. It would never be something that we would wish upon our worst enemy, but it was something that was given to us without reserve. What a gift for her to be able to see that so clearly already. Now I had to help her come to a place where she could see that this cross was given as a beautiful, glorious gift. Easter is coming.

Mass Moments

Good Friday is a pretty intense service. Look over this chapter and think about the things you want to look for, remember, or appreciate as you attend Mass on Good Friday. Write them down on the pages in the back.

CHAPTER 5

Holy Saturday: Waiting, Remembering, Rejoicing

When I was a child, one of the best parts of Christmas was going to sleep on Christmas Eve. The anticipation of Santa's arrival was almost more than I could bear. I just knew that in the morning, there would be cookie crumbs on the plate, a half-drunk glass of milk, and presents spilling out from under the tree for my three siblings and me. The waiting was hard, but it was worth it. I would struggle through the excitement to go to sleep because if I didn't sleep, Santa couldn't come.

As an adult, Holy Saturday holds a similar appeal for me. As we begin in darkness and sorrow, I know that a glorious moment is coming soon. When I have been able to place myself fully in the celebrations of the previous week, the anticipation of the return of the light is almost more than I can take. I am ready for this heaviness to be lifted. I am ready for this weight be given purpose and meaning. I hope you are, too.

Preparation

As we return to the church, there is a striking contrast from the night before. Flowers fill the church, and the purple and red of Lent is gone, replaced by white everywhere you look. The vestments are white, the flowers are white, and the candles are white. Everything is bright and beautiful. However, we are not quite ready. The lights are off, and darkness covers the beauty. It is not yet time.

Entry

As we did on Palm Sunday, we begin this service outside of the church. This time, the priest blesses a fire. The flames provide warmth and dispel the surrounding darkness. From this blessed fire, the Paschal candle is lit. The Paschal Candle is a symbol of the light of Christ that scatters the "darkness of our hearts and minds" as proclaimed by the priest at the lighting. This candle will be used throughout the year in baptisms, funerals, and other services to remind us of the presence of Christ within them. It will also be lit during each Mass of the Easter season, reminding us that Jesus was physically present on earth until the Pentecost.

The candle is processed in and proclaimed three times on the way to the altar: once at the door of the altar, once in the middle of the church, and once at the foot of the altar. We did the same procession with the cross yesterday. Three times we lifted the cross and revealed the instrument of Jesus' death. Today we lift the candle three times, showing how the light of Christ has overcome the darkness of the cross.

As a part of the entrance, there will be people processing in behind the priest. It may be the entire congregation, or it may just be the people who will be entering the Catholic faith today. Either way, the light of Christ leads them just as the fire of God led the Israelites as they wandered at night through the desert on the way to the Promised Land.[1]

---

[1] EXODUS 13:21-22

> *From there, the light is passed until each person's candle is glowing. This church that sits in darkness is filled with the light of Christ as one person passes it to another.*

As the candle comes to the middle of the church, the altar servers and clergy will light their candles from the Paschal candle and pass their light onto the people at the end of the aisles. From there, the light is passed until each person's candle is glowing. This church that sits in darkness is filled with the light of Christ as one person passes it to another. This is one of my favorite parts of Holy Saturday. The light that fills the room is much brighter than it seems it should be given the size of the candles we hold. It is a beautiful, soft light that spreads little by little, enveloping each person in the warmth of its glow.

After the Paschal candle reaches the altar, it is placed in its holder, the lights of the church are turned on, and the Easter Proclamation is announced. The light of Christ has returned, and the Proclamation summarizes all that has led to this moment. It is a preview of what we will hear in the readings tonight. We are to remember that this moment comes as part of a much larger story. Without the rest of the story, the meaning of this moment is lost.

Some churches will leave the lights off until right before the Gloria. After the final Old Testament reading, the lights are turned on, and the altar candles are lit. The darkness that surrounds the readings of the Old Testament is lifted at the moment when we enter into the New Testament and proclaim Jesus' Resurrection.

Food for Thought

1. Many times in our lives, blessings are hidden in moments of sorrow or suffering. Can you remember a time when you discovered a blessing that had been hidden from view?

2. As we pass the flame of our candles from person to person, we are reminded that we pass the light of Christ to each other. Lighting a candle is such a simple action. What are some simple ways that you can share the light of Christ with those around you, whether in church or outside of church?

First Reading *Genesis 1:1-2:2*

On Holy Saturday, there are seven Old Testament and two New Testament readings. Given the time it takes to go through all of them, churches are allowed to decrease the number of Old Testament readings to three. We, however, will go through all of the readings. Just as the Easter Proclamation led us through our salvation history, these passages of scripture help us to see what is being accomplished today much more clearly. If we ever think that we can neglect or ignore the Old Testament as something that has been replaced by the New, this

Mass shows us that the Church believes that the opposite is true. The Old Testament is important and key to our understanding of the New, and it is to be revered as much as the New Testament writings.

- *Genesis 1:1—2:2 (short version Genesis 1:1, 26-31A)*

    In the beginning, when God created the heavens and the earth, the earth was a formless wasteland, and darkness covered the abyss, while a mighty wind swept over the waters.

    Then God said, "Let there be light," and there was light. God saw how good the light was. God then separated the light from the darkness. God called the light "day," and the darkness he called "night." Thus evening came, and morning followed—the first day.

    Then God said, "Let there be a dome in the middle of the waters, to separate one body of water from the other." And so it happened: God made the dome, and it separated the water above the dome from the water below it. God called the dome "the sky." Evening came, and morning followed—the second day.

    Then God said, "Let the water under the sky be gathered into a single basin, so that the dry land may appear." And so it happened: the water under the sky was gathered into its basin, and the dry land appeared. God called the dry land "the earth, " and the basin of the water he called "the sea." God saw how good it was. Then God said, "Let the earth bring forth vegetation: every kind of plant that bears seed and every kind of fruit tree on earth that bears fruit with its seed in it." And so it happened: the earth brought forth every kind of plant that bears seed and every kind of fruit tree on earth that bears fruit with its seed in it. God saw how good it was. Evening came, and morning followed—the third day.

    Then God said: "Let there be lights in the dome of the sky, to separate day from night. Let them mark the fixed times, the days and the years, and serve as luminaries in the dome of the sky, to shed light upon the earth." And so it happened: God made the two great lights, the greater one to govern the day, and the lesser one to govern the night; and he made the stars. God set them in the dome of the sky, to shed light upon the earth, to govern the day and the night, and to separate the light from the darkness. God saw how good it was. Evening came, and morning followed—the fourth day.

Then God said, "Let the water teem with an abundance of living creatures, and on the earth let birds fly beneath the dome of the sky." And so it happened: God created the great sea monsters and all kinds of swimming creatures with which the water teems, and all kinds of winged birds. God saw how good it was, and God blessed them, saying, "Be fertile, multiply, and fill the water of the seas; and let the birds multiply on the earth." Evening came, and morning followed— the fifth day.

Then God said, "Let the earth bring forth all kinds of living creatures: cattle, creeping things, and wild animals of all kinds." And so it happened: God made all kinds of wild animals, all kinds of cattle, and all kinds of creeping things of the earth. God saw how good it was. Then God said:

"Let us make man in our image, after our likeness. Let them have dominion over the fish of the sea, the birds of the air, and the cattle, and over all the wild animals and all the creatures that crawl on the ground."

> *God created man in his image;*
> *in the image of God he created him;*
> *male and female he created them.*

God blessed them, saying: "Be fertile and multiply; fill the earth and subdue it. Have dominion over the fish of the sea, the birds of the air, and all the living things that move on the earth." God also said: "See, I give you every seed-bearing plant all over the earth and every tree that has seed-bearing fruit on it to be your food; and to all the animals of the land, all the birds of the air, and all the living creatures that crawl on the ground, I give all the green plants for food." And so it happened. God looked at everything he had made, and he found it very good. Evening came, and morning followed—the sixth day.

Thus the heavens and the earth and all their array were completed. Since on the seventh day God was finished with the work he had been doing, he rested on the seventh day from all the work he had undertaken.

We have heard this story before. God created the world in six days, and on the seventh day He rested. It is a beautiful piece of poetry, which we can glimpse in our translations from the original. The structure can tell us a bit about the meaning. Each day, we see "Then God said," "And so it happened," "God saw how good it was," and "evening came and morning followed." Each of these can tell us something about the creative character of God.

1. **"Then God said"** - To create something, all that needs to happen is for God to say it. The power of His word is the power of life.

2. **"And so it happened"** - As God says, so it is. Not something similar to what He says; it is exactly as He says.

3. **"God saw how good it was"** - God's creation is good. The sea, the sky, the plants, the animals, and each one of us. As God looked at the entirety of His creation and the balance within it, He saw that it was "very good."

4. **"Evening came and morning followed"** – God's creation takes place over time. He could have spoken all of creation into existence in a moment, but instead chose to work it through, allowing each thing to lead to the next. We can be patient knowing that "He who started a good work in [us] will continue to complete it until the day of Christ Jesus." (Phil 1:6)

Responsorial Psalm *Psalm 104:1-2, 5-6, 10, 12, 13-14, 24, 35*

After each reading today, there will be a Psalm that is connected directly to the scripture that has just been read. Look for the connections in each one. Some of them are quite poignant. In this one, we reflect and sing of the wonders of God's creation. He has created the earth, and we ask for Him to renew it again.

- *Psalm 104: 1-2, 5-6, 10, 12, 13-14, 24, 35* [1]

    R. (30) Lord, send out your Spirit, and renew the face of the earth.

    Bless the LORD, O my soul!
    O LORD, my God, you are great indeed!
    You are clothed with majesty and glory,
    robed in light as with a cloak.

    R. Lord, send out your Spirit, and renew the face of the earth.

    You fixed the earth upon its foundation,
    not to be moved forever;
    with the ocean, as with a garment, you covered it;
    above the mountains the waters stood.

    R. Lord, send out your Spirit, and renew the face of the earth.

    You send forth springs into the watercourses
    that wind among the mountains.
    Beside them the birds of heaven dwell;
    from among the branches they send forth their song.

    R. Lord, send out your Spirit, and renew the face of the earth.

    You water the mountains from your palace;
    the earth is replete with the fruit of your works.
    You raise grass for the cattle,
    and vegetation for man's use,
    producing bread from the earth.

    R. Lord, send out your Spirit, and renew the face of the earth.

---

[1] ALTERNATE READING IS FOUND IN APPENDIX A

How manifold are your works, O LORD!
  In wisdom you have wrought them all
—the earth is full of your creatures.
  Bless the LORD, O my soul!.

R. Lord, send out your Spirit, and renew the face of the earth.

Many people say that they experience God in nature. This is the perfect Psalm for them. It sings of the wonders of God's creation. For all of us, it is a reminder that we are given glimpses of God every day. We are surrounded by the works of His hands. May we never stop at the admiration of the beauty of a sunset or the majesty of a mountain. May we always see beyond the creation to stand in wonder of the Creator who made it.

Food for Thought

1. Do you believe that God has the power to create with a word? Why or why not?

2. Describe a time when you have seen God in nature. How did it affect you?

3. Look up right now, where you are. If you can't see or hear some part of God's creation, get to where you can, and write down something wonderful that you recognize in it.

Second Reading *Genesis 22:1-18*

This is one of my favorite stories in the Bible. When God was opening up my faith, it was here that I started to see the Bible in an entirely different way. As you read this passage, remember that it is here as part of the story of Jesus. As St. Augustine says, "The New Testament lies hidden in the Old, and the Old Testament is unveiled in the New." We have already looked at this passage in our discussion of the Second Station of the Cross. See what else you can discover hidden in this story.

- *Genesis 22:1-18 (Short version: Genesis 22:1-2, 9A, 10-13, 15-18)*

    God put Abraham to the test. He called to him, "Abraham!" "Here I am," he replied. Then God said: "Take your son Isaac, your only one, whom you love, and go to the land of Moriah. There you shall offer him up as a holocaust on a height that I will point out to you." Early the next morning Abraham saddled his donkey, took with him his son Isaac and two of his servants as well, and with the wood that he had cut for the holocaust, set out for the place of which God had told him.

    On the third day Abraham got sight of the place from afar. Then he said to his servants: "Both of you stay here with the donkey, while the boy and I go on over yonder. We will worship and then come back to you." Thereupon Abraham took the wood for the holocaust and laid it on his son Isaac's shoulders, while he himself carried the fire and the knife. As the two walked on together, Isaac spoke to his father Abraham: "Father!" Isaac said. "Yes, son, " he replied. Isaac continued, "Here are the fire and the wood, but where is the sheep for the holocaust?" "Son," Abraham answered, "God himself will provide the sheep for the holocaust." Then the two continued going forward.

When they came to the place of which God had told him, Abraham built an altar there and arranged the wood on it. Next he tied up his son Isaac, and put him on top of the wood on the altar. Then he reached out and took the knife to slaughter his son. But the LORD's messenger called to him from heaven, "Abraham, Abraham!" "Here I am!" he answered. "Do not lay your hand on the boy," said the messenger. "Do not do the least thing to him. I know now how devoted you are to God, since you did not withhold from me your own beloved son." As Abraham looked about, he spied a ram caught by its horns in the thicket. So he went and took the ram and offered it up as a holocaust in place of his son. Abraham named the site Yahweh-yireh; hence people now say, "On the mountain the LORD will see."

Again the LORD's messenger called to Abraham from heaven and said: "I swear by myself, declares the LORD, that because you acted as you did in not withholding from me your beloved son, I will bless you abundantly and make your descendants as countless as the stars of the sky and the sands of the seashore; your descendants shall take possession of the gates of their enemies, and in your descendants all the nations of the earth shall find blessing, all this because you obeyed my command."

So often, we can look back at our lives and see how God has orchestrated events perfectly. In the moment, we may be confused, we may misunderstand, and we may see our situation as something useless or pointless. In our readings today, we are given a reminder that God's plan can take a very long time, but that doesn't mean that God isn't working in it the entire time.

Food for Thought

1. What were some of the parallels to Jesus that you found in the story? (I've listed some in Appendix D for reference)

2. Just as we saw in the Gospel reading on Good Friday, Abraham proclaims the truth without even knowing that he does so – "God will provide the sheep for the holocaust." Do you think that we often speak the truth without truly understanding what we are saying?

3. Many people like to keep a journal of some type. What would be the benefit of looking back on our lives of faith and seeing how God has led us to where we are?

> **SPEAKING MY LANGUAGE**
>
> As a Texan, I love the fact that "you stay here with the donkey, while the boy and I go over yonder," is a quote from the Bible. They just need to add "y'all" to make me feel right at home. A little connection for me as I'm fixin' to celebrate Easter.

RESURRECTION COOKIES (FOR SATURDAY)

A fun, family Easter tradition is to make these cookies that tell the story of Easter. Before you go to Holy Saturday Mass, make these cookies, and leave them to cook until Easter morning.

Ingredients:

1 c. whole pecans
1 tsp. white vinegar
3 egg whites
pinch salt
1 c. sugar
zipper baggie
tape
Bible

1. Preheat the oven to 300° F.
2. Place the pecans in zipper baggie and let the children beat them with a wooden spoon to break the small pieces.

   Explain that after Jesus was arrested, He was beaten by the Roman soldiers. Read John 19:1-3.

3. Let each child smell the vinegar. Put 1 tsp. vinegar into the mixing bowl.

   Explain that when Jesus was thirsty on the cross, he was given vinegar to drink. Read John 19:28-30.

4. Add egg whites to the vinegar. Eggs represent life.

   Explain that Jesus gave His life to give us life. Read John 10:10-11

5. Sprinkle a little salt into each child's hand. Let them taste it and brush the rest into the bowl.

   Explain that this represents the salty tears shed by Jesus' followers, and the bitterness of our own sin. Read Luke 23:27.

6. So far the ingredients are not very appetizing. Add 1 c. sugar.

   Explain that the sweetest part of the story is that Jesus died because He loves us. He wants to know and belong to Him. Read Psalm 34:8 and John 3:16-17.

(continued)

(continued)

7. **Beat with a mixer on high speed for 12-15 minutes until stiff peaks are formed.**

   Explain that, in God's eyes, the color white represents the purity of those whose sins have been cleansed by Jesus. Read Isaiah 1:18 and John 3:1-3.

8. **Fold in the broken nuts. Drop by teaspoons onto a wax paper or parchment paper covered cookie sheet.**

   Explain that each mound represents the rocky tomb where Jesus' body was laid. Read Matthew 27:57-60.

9. **Put the cookie sheet in the oven, close the door and turn the oven OFF.**

10. **Give each child a piece of tape and seal the oven door.**

    Explain that Jesus' tomb was sealed. Read Matthew 27:65-66.

11. **Go to bed!**

    Explain that they may feel sad to leave the cookies in the oven overnight. Jesus' followers were in despair when the tomb was sealed. Read John 16:20 and 22.

12. **On Easter morning, open the oven and give everyone a cookie. Notice the cracked surface and take a bite. The cookies are hollow!**

    On the first Easter, Jesus' followers were amazed to find the tomb open and empty. Read Matthew 28:1-9.

Responsorial Psalm

Psalm 16:5, 8, 9-10, 11

Imagine what you would feel if you came within seconds of sacrificing your son, and received him back again, safe and sound. Child sacrifice was not unknown at this time in the Bible, but it still must have been difficult for any parent asked to give up a child. As God refused to accept the sacrifice of Isaac, how would Abraham's understanding change? This God is different from the gods that Abraham knows—radically different. He has shown that death is not what He desires. He desires a heart that is willing to give everything to Him. If we offer everything to God, He shows us here that He will not destroy it, but instead will bring life and give it back to us. As we sing this Psalm, we are reminded of this new understanding. How can we keep from singing?

■ *Psalm 16:5, 8, 9-10, 11*

R. (1) You are my inheritance, O Lord.

O LORD, my allotted portion and my cup,
 you it is who hold fast my lot.
I set the LORD ever before me;
 with him at my right hand I shall not be disturbed.

R. You are my inheritance, O Lord.

Therefore my heart is glad and my soul rejoices,
 my body, too, abides in confidence;
because you will not abandon my soul to the netherworld,
 nor will you suffer your faithful one to undergo corruption.

R. You are my inheritance, O Lord.

You will show me the path to life,
 fullness of joys in your presence,
 the delights at your right hand forever.

R. You are my inheritance, O Lord.

Food for Thought

1. What is something that you try to keep from God, or where is a place in your life that you refuse to let Him in?

2. If you could trust that God would bring life into that place instead of destroying it, what could happen?

3. Can you invite God in now? Try it.

Third Reading

Exodus 14:15-15:1

This next story is very familiar to us. The crossing of the Red Sea has been the topic of movies, it is the subject of cartoons, and it is a part of the general culture. On Holy Saturday, we remember this moment of deliverance, and we see how it leads to the cross.

As we enter the story, the Israelites are trapped, cornered by an army that just won't let them go. Pharaoh has offered to let them go a few times before, but each time he changes his mind. This time was no different. The Israelites are in a panic and have asked Moses to call out for help. We start with God's almost casual response to the request.

■ *Exodus 14:15-15:1*

> *The LORD said to Moses, "Why are you crying out to me? Tell the Israelites to go forward. And you, lift up your staff and, with hand outstretched over the sea, split the sea in two, that the Israelites may pass through it on dry land. But I will make the Egyptians so obstinate that they will go in after them. Then I will receive glory through Pharaoh and all his army, his chariots and charioteers. The Egyptians shall know that I am the LORD, when I receive glory through Pharaoh and his chariots and charioteers."*
>
> *The angel of God, who had been leading Israel's camp, now moved and went around behind them. The column of cloud also, leaving the front, took up its place behind them, so that it came between the camp of the Egyptians and that of Israel. But the cloud now became dark, and thus the night passed without the rival camps coming any closer together all night long. Then Moses stretched out his hand over the sea, and the LORD swept the sea with a strong east wind throughout the night and so turned it into dry land. When the water was thus divided, the Israelites marched into the midst of the sea on dry land, with the water like a wall to their right and to their left.*

The Israelites marched into the midst of the sea on dry land, with the water like a wall to their right and to their left

The Egyptians followed in pursuit; all Pharaoh's horses and chariots and charioteers went after them right into the midst of the sea. In the night watch just before dawn, the LORD cast through the column of the fiery cloud upon the Egyptian force a glance that threw it into a panic; and he so clogged their chariot wheels that they could hardly drive. With that the Egyptians sounded the retreat before Israel, because the LORD was fighting for them against the Egyptians.

Then the LORD told Moses, "Stretch out your hand over the sea, that the water may flow back upon the Egyptians, upon their chariots and their charioteers." So Moses stretched out his hand over the sea, and at dawn the sea flowed back to its normal depth. The Egyptians were fleeing head on toward the sea, when the LORD hurled them into its midst. As the water flowed back, it covered the chariots and the charioteers of Pharaoh's whole army which had followed the Israelites into the sea. Not a single one of them escaped. But the Israelites had marched on dry land through the midst of the sea, with the water like a wall to their right and to their left. Thus the LORD saved Israel on that day from the power of the Egyptians. When Israel saw the Egyptians lying dead on the seashore and beheld the great power that the LORD had shown against the Egyptians, they feared the LORD and believed in him and in his servant Moses.

Then Moses and the Israelites sang this song to the LORD:
   I will sing to the LORD, for he is gloriously triumphant;
   horse and chariot he has cast into the sea.

In this reading, the waters of the Red Sea show us that we can be freed from slavery. At the same time, the waters prefigure the waters of baptism that free us from sin. The insistent captors remind us of the ever-present temptation of sin. Sin is not gone because we have been baptized, but the miraculous path created through the sea reminds us that God has the power to bring us through and deliver us from evil. We have seen, and we will remember.

Food for Thought

1. Describe a time when God has stepped in to fix a situation in your life – whether in a perfectly timed offer for help, by opening a door that should have been closed, or some other action.

2. Part of receiving a blessing is the ability to accept it. How easy or hard was it for you to accept this gift?

The Israelites needed to be taken from Egypt so that their gaze would not turn from God. He will show His devotion again and again. Even so, it will not be enough.

Responsorial Psalm *Exodus 15:1-2, 3-4, 5-6, 17-18*

You may notice that this Psalm is not actually a Psalm at all. It is a continuation of the reading we just finished, and it is the song that is referenced in the last verse.

This story can be a little difficult for those of us who are not comfortable with war. It is easy to ask why God would kill this army as we sit in our comfortable chairs in our comfortable homes. It is a good question, and one that we should not presume to answer by placing the people of the Bible into the culture of today. In Biblical times, the security of a nation was hard fought and needed constant protection. The Israelites knew that the Egyptian army was not going to negotiate, and it was not going to give up. This had been made quite clear.

At the same time, the Israelites needed to be taken from Egypt with no chance of returning so that their gaze would not turn from God. God had shown His power through the plagues and their release from slavery. Here He shows that He is with them, even in their freedom. He will show His devotion again and again. Even so, it will not be enough.

As we look forward to Jesus, we are reminded that our sins may have been forgiven, but it doesn't mean that they don't have power over us. We have been freed, but we can still be pursued. The work of Jesus isn't complete on Good Friday. It continues to Easter Sunday and well beyond. Of that we can be sure.

■ *Exodus 15:1-2, 3-4, 5-6, 17-18*

R. (1b) Let us sing to the Lord; he has covered himself in glory.

I will sing to the LORD, for he is gloriously triumphant;
 horse and chariot he has cast into the sea.
My strength and my courage is the LORD,
 and he has been my savior.
He is my God, I praise him;
 the God of my father, I extol him.

R. Let us sing to the Lord; he has covered himself in glory.

The LORD is a warrior,
 LORD is his name!
Pharaoh's chariots and army he hurled into the sea;
 the elite of his officers were submerged in the Red Sea.

R. Let us sing to the Lord; he has covered himself in glory.

The flood waters covered them,
 they sank into the depths like a stone.
Your right hand, O LORD, magnificent in power,
 your right hand, O LORD, has shattered the enemy.

R. Let us sing to the Lord; he has covered himself in glory.

You brought in the people you redeemed
 and planted them on the mountain of your inheritance—
the place where you made your seat, O LORD,
 the sanctuary, LORD, which your hands established.
The LORD shall reign forever and ever.

R. Let us sing to the Lord; he has covered himself in glory.

Food for Thought

1. Do you have something that is pursuing you? A burden that you can't put down?

2. We can rarely work through a difficult situation quickly. How do you see God working in this situation?

3. What praise can you offer to God for the work He has done already?

Fourth Reading
Isaiah 54:5-14

The next reading comes as Israel returns from exile. After many years in the desert, they arrived at the Promised Land and established a nation. Years later they turned from God in drastic ways. They worshipped other gods, placed idols in the Temple, and their lives were in direct conflict with the commands God had given to preserve them and bring them closer to Him. They were far away from the life God wanted for them.

God allowed the exile to help the Israelites see physically where they were spiritually. In exile, they could find their desire to return, and in these readings, God is bringing them home. He loves them so much, and He swears that His love will never leave them.

■ *Isaiah 54:5-14*

> The One who has become your husband is your Maker;
>   his name is the LORD of hosts;
> your redeemer is the Holy One of Israel,
>   called God of all the earth.
> The LORD calls you back,
>   like a wife forsaken and grieved in spirit,
>   a wife married in youth and then cast off,
>   says your God.
> For a brief moment I abandoned you,
>   but with great tenderness I will take you back.
> In an outburst of wrath, for a moment
>   I hid my face from you;
> but with enduring love I take pity on you,
>   says the LORD, your redeemer.
> This is for me like the days of Noah,
>   when I swore that the waters of Noah
>   should never again deluge the earth;
> so I have sworn not to be angry with you,
>   or to rebuke you.
> Though the mountains leave their place
>   and the hills be shaken,

my love shall never leave you
    nor my covenant of peace be shaken,
    says the LORD, who has mercy on you.
O afflicted one, storm-battered and unconsoled,
    I lay your pavements in carnelians,
    and your foundations in sapphires;
I will make your battlements of rubies,
    your gates of carbuncles,
    and all your walls of precious stones.
All your children shall be taught by the LORD,
    and great shall be the peace of your children.
In justice shall you be established,
    far from the fear of oppression,
    where destruction cannot come near you.

It is hard to see that correction or punishment is a sign of love, but we are to remember that this punishment is to help the Israelites find their way back. They would never have seen their transgressions if they had stayed in the Promised Land. We are to believe when God says,

For my thoughts are not your thoughts,
    nor are your ways my ways, says the LORD.
As high as the heavens are above the earth,
    so high are my ways above your ways
    and my thoughts above your thoughts.

For just as from the heavens
    the rain and snow come down
and do not return there
    till they have watered the earth,
    making it fertile and fruitful,
giving seed to the one who sows
    and bread to the one who eats,
so shall my word be
    that goes forth from my mouth;

my word shall not return to me void,
   but shall do my will,
      achieving the end for which I sent it. (Isaiah 55:8-11)

The word of God was not of abandonment, but a plea for return. In these readings, it has been accomplished.

    Just like any other parent, I have had to punish my children. It is never easy, and I can say that I am so joyful when the punishment has the effect of helping them return to the right path. I love when the lesson is learned, and I can hold them again in a strong, loving, warm embrace. The thing I love most about this reading is the beautiful return that is offered to those who have wandered. God's tenderness is incredibly touching. I relish sitting with these words and feeling His love surround me, no matter what I have done.

Responsorial Psalm *Psalm 30: 2, 4, 5-6, 11-12, 13*

As I mentioned at the beginning of this chapter, each Responsorial Psalm is directly linked to the reading before it. As we read this one, listen as the people who have just returned from exile acknowledge that it was God who brought them home.

■ *Psalm 30: 2, 4, 5-6, 11-12, 13*

    R. (2a) I will praise you, Lord, for you have rescued me.

I will extol you, O LORD, for you drew me clear
   and did not let my enemies rejoice over me.
O LORD, you brought me up from the netherworld;
   you preserved me from among those going down into the pit.

    R. I will praise you, Lord, for you have rescued me.

Sing praise to the LORD, you his faithful ones,
   and give thanks to his holy name.
For his anger lasts but a moment;
   a lifetime, his good will.

At nightfall, weeping enters in,
   but with the dawn, rejoicing.

R. I will praise you, Lord, for you have rescued me.

Hear, O LORD, and have pity on me;
   O LORD, be my helper.
You changed my mourning into dancing;
   O LORD, my God, forever will I give you thanks.

R. I will praise you, Lord, for you have rescued me.

Now I want you to read the Responsorial Psalm a second time. The first time, we read it as it was meant in the moment. We've learned that nothing in the Old Testament is quite that simple, so I want you to read it again in the context of Holy Week and Easter. This time we know that Jesus has died and that, in a moment, we will see His resurrection.

Food for Thought

1. Many of us make requests in prayer, but few of us acknowledge when they are answered. Is there a prayer that has been answered recently that you should say thank you for? Say it now.

2. When you read the Psalm a second time, how did the meaning change? What stood out the most for you and why?

Fifth Reading *Isaiah 55:1-11*

Once again, we have an Old Testament reading that gives us insight into Jesus. As you read this passage, be sure to notice the connections between the two. Isaiah says that we don't need bread, but that we will eat rich fare with the Lord. The covenant will be renewed, and nations other than Israel will be drawn to Him. All of us are invited, and it doesn't matter who we are, what we have done, or how much we own.

■ *Isaiah 55:1-11*

> Thus says the LORD:
> All you who are thirsty,
>   come to the water!
> You who have no money,
>   come, receive grain and eat;
> come, without paying and without cost,
>   drink wine and milk!
> Why spend your money for what is not bread,
>   your wages for what fails to satisfy?
> Heed me, and you shall eat well,
>   you shall delight in rich fare.
> Come to me heedfully,
>   listen, that you may have life.
> I will renew with you the everlasting covenant,
>   the benefits assured to David.
> As I made him a witness to the peoples,
>   a leader and commander of nations,
> so shall you summon a nation you knew not,
>   and nations that knew you not shall run to you,
> because of the LORD, your God,
>   the Holy One of Israel, who has glorified you.

Seek the LORD while he may be found,
　　call him while he is near.
Let the scoundrel forsake his way,
　　and the wicked man his thoughts;
let him turn to the LORD for mercy;
　　to our God, who is generous in forgiving.
For my thoughts are not your thoughts,
　　nor are your ways my ways, says the LORD.
As high as the heavens are above the earth,
　　so high are my ways above your ways
　　and my thoughts above your thoughts.

For just as from the heavens
　　the rain and snow come down
and do not return there
　　till they have watered the earth,
　　making it fertile and fruitful,
giving seed to the one who sows
　　and bread to the one who eats,
so shall my word be
　　that goes forth from my mouth;
my word shall not return to me void,
　　but shall do my will,
　　achieving the end for which I sent it.

Seek the Lord while he may be found, call him while he is near

This reading is the only one today that is not addressing a specific event in the history of salvation. Instead, it is God's call for all of us to come to Him. We are not to worry about money, our past, or even the thought of a cruel and vengeful God. It is the invitation that we have been given all along. As we approach the dawn of Easter, may it ring loudly in our hearts.

Food for Thought

1. What part of this reading speaks to you today?

2. What is God saying to you in it?

3. What is your response?

Responsorial Psalm

Isaiah 12:2-3, 4, 5-6

This Responsorial Psalm is taken from Isaiah. Continuing the theme of water, it gives us a peek into the power of water in salvation. We've seen these waters all week, and we will see them soon in the baptisms that will be performed tonight. This is the water of the last reading: "All who are thirsty, come to the water!" (Isaiah 55:1)

- *Isaiah 12:2-3, 4, 5-6*

    R. (3) You will draw water joyfully from the springs of salvation.

    God indeed is my savior;
    *   I am confident and unafraid.*
    My strength and my courage is the LORD,
    *   and he has been my savior.*
    With joy you will draw water
    *   at the fountain of salvation.*

    R. You will draw water joyfully from the springs of salvation.

    Give thanks to the LORD, acclaim his name;
    *   among the nations make known his deeds,*
    *   proclaim how exalted is his name.*

    R. You will draw water joyfully from the springs of salvation.

    Sing praise to the LORD for his glorious achievement;
    *   let this be known throughout all the earth.*
    Shout with exultation, O city of Zion,
    *   for great in your midst*
    *   is the Holy One of Israel!*

    R. You will draw water joyfully from the springs of salvation.

Food for Thought

1. The verse before this Response explains that these are the words the people of God will sing when they are saved from exile. How do you praise or thank God when you have been blessed?

2. List a couple of blessings in your life, and thank God for them here.

Sixth Reading *Baruch 3:9-15, 3:32-4:4*

Right after we hear of the Israelites' return from exile, we see that they are falling again. Baruch and the next Psalm remind us that we already "have the words of everlasting life," but just as the Israelites forgot, we can forget. We get distracted, discouraged, frightened, or busy. We decide that we will work on our faith later, when we have more time, or we don't feel like our faith is doing much for us anyway. Before we know it, we have wandered away from the words of life and are in the land of the dead. We are being invited back, again and again. We are invited to a life of peace, wisdom, and joy. Israel was invited then, and we are invited now. Hear, and believe.

- *Baruch 3:9-15, 3:32-4:4*

    Hear, O Israel, the commandments of life:
        listen, and know prudence!
    How is it, Israel,
        that you are in the land of your foes,
        grown old in a foreign land,
    defiled with the dead,
        accounted with those destined for the netherworld?
    You have forsaken the fountain of wisdom!
        Had you walked in the way of God,
        you would have dwelt in enduring peace.
    Learn where prudence is,
        where strength, where understanding;
    that you may know also
        where are length of days, and life,
        where light of the eyes, and peace.
    Who has found the place of wisdom,
        who has entered into her treasuries?

    The One who knows all things knows her;
        he has probed her by his knowledge.
    The One who established the earth for all time,
        and filled it with four-footed beasts;
    he who dismisses the light, and it departs,
        calls it, and it obeys him trembling;
    before whom the stars at their posts
        shine and rejoice;
    when he calls them, they answer, "Here we are!"
        shining with joy for their Maker.
    Such is our God;
        no other is to be compared to him:
    he has traced out the whole way of understanding,
        and has given her to Jacob, his servant,
        to Israel, his beloved son.

Since then she has appeared on earth,
*   and moved among people.*
She is the book of the precepts of God,
*   the law that endures forever;*
all who cling to her will live,
*   but those will die who forsake her.*
Turn, O Jacob, and receive her:
*   walk by her light toward splendor.*
Give not your glory to another,
*   your privileges to an alien race.*
Blessed are we, O Israel;
*   for what pleases God is known to us!*

My favorite verse in this passage is about the stars at their posts. "When he calls them, they answer, 'Here we are!'/ shining with joy for their Maker." (Baruch 3:35) It makes me think of when my children were little. As we played outside, they would come running when I called them over to where I was, knowing that they could expect a wonderful surprise. It might be a delicious treat, a weird bug, or some new adventure, but they were shining with joy in anticipation of the effect of the call.

    How often do we run with joy as God is calling us? How often do we shine with joy for our Maker? This reading reminds us to capture and remain in that joy so that we don't end up in exile.

> *Just as the Israelites forgot, we can forget. Before we know it, we have wandered away from the words of life and are in the land of the dead*

Holy Saturday

Food for Thought

1. God's laws are rarely seen as "commandments for life" today. How do you think they could be life-giving rather than restrictive?

2. Have you had a moment of joy for your Maker? What was it about? What does it tell you about your relationship with God?

3. How could focusing on that joy help you to obey God's commands?

Responsorial Psalm *Psalm 19:8, 9, 10, 11*

As we read through this Psalm, we are reminded of the previous reading and the "commandments for life." In general, we balk against rules. Actually, we like rules for other people or ones that protect our personal interests, but we don't usually like rules that affect what we want to do. They restrict us, impose on our freedom, and deny our ability to follow our passions. Somehow, though, the Psalmist sees them as refreshing, life-giving, and desirable. Note the characteristics and effects of the Law as they are listed here. We'll discuss them in a moment.

- *Psalm 19:8, 9, 10, 11*

    R. (John 6:68c) Lord, you have the words of everlasting life.

    The law of the LORD is perfect,
      refreshing the soul;
    the decree of the LORD is trustworthy,
      giving wisdom to the simple.

    R. Lord, you have the words of everlasting life.

    The precepts of the LORD are right,
      rejoicing the heart;
    the command of the LORD is clear,
      enlightening the eye.

    R. Lord, you have the words of everlasting life.

    The fear of the LORD is pure,
      enduring forever;
    the ordinances of the LORD are true,
      all of them just.

    R. Lord, you have the words of everlasting life.

They are more precious than gold,
  than a heap of purest gold;
sweeter also than syrup
  or honey from the comb.

R. Lord, you have the words of everlasting life.

The law is sweet, precious, and gives joy and wisdom. These are not usually the terms we would use to describe the law. They give order, promote peace, and provide control. These are more consistent descriptions of our understandings. If we just look at one commandment, however, we can see that it is not just about providing order and control.

If the entire world lived by the commandment, "Thou shalt not kill," what would it look like? If all of us not only refused to kill, but fulfilled that law as Jesus described in Matthew 5:21-26—understanding that the killing starts with hatred, anger, and lack of forgiveness – what would the world be like? Prohibiting murder is a measure of control for a society, but the law of God is not about control. It is about freeing us from the things that distort us. It is about allowing us to live as a reflection of the love that God has for us. In that, we are free. In that, we are fulfilled. In that are the words of everlasting life.

YOU'VE GOT IT ALL BACKWARDS

As he was coming into a life of faith, my husband struggled with his understanding of a controlling God. One of his main focal points was the Ten Commandments. For him, they were unreasonable entry requirements for an exclusive club. "Worship Me, and Me only, and I will let you in," was the message that he heard. We wrestled with this for quite a while until I saw that we were coming at them from the absolute wrong direction.

What if we were looking at them backwards? What if they weren't payment for a restricted entry, but keys to open the door? With this new perspective, we could see that God wasn't telling us, "Do this, or I won't love you," but was saying, "Do these so you can live in the love I have for you." It changed my husband's faith immediately, and the door opened wider than he had ever imagined it could.

Food for Thought

1. What words of God are speaking to you in this Psalm?

2. How are they drawing you to the "land of the living?"

Seventh Reading *Ezekiel 36:16-17a, 18-28*

The seventh reading offers hope for return from the exile just addressed in the sixth reading from Baruch. An interesting thing to note here is that neither one of these readings talks about how the Israelites have repented or turned away from their sins. Yet God will return them to their land to show His mercy and power.

- *Ezekiel 36:16-17a, 18-28*

    The word of the LORD came to me, saying: Son of man, when the house of Israel lived in their land, they defiled it by their conduct and deeds. Therefore I poured out my fury upon them because of the blood that they poured out on the ground, and because they defiled it with idols. I scattered them among the nations, dispersing them over foreign lands; according to their conduct and deeds I judged them. But when they came among the nations wherever they came, they served to profane my holy name, because it was said of them: "These are the people of the LORD, yet they had to leave their land." So I have relented because of my holy name which the house of Israel profaned among the nations where they came. Therefore say to the house of Israel: Thus says the Lord GOD: Not for your sakes do I act, house of Israel, but for the sake of my holy name, which you profaned among the nations to which you came. I will prove the holiness of my great name, profaned among the nations, in whose midst you have profaned it. Thus the nations shall know that I am the LORD, says the Lord GOD, when in their sight I prove my holiness through you. For I will take you away from among the nations, gather you from all the foreign lands, and bring you back to your own land. I will sprinkle clean water upon you to cleanse you from all your impurities, and from all your idols I will cleanse you. I will give you a new heart and place a new spirit within you, taking from your bodies your stony hearts and giving you natural hearts. I will put my spirit within you and make you live by my statutes, careful to observe my decrees. You shall live in the land I gave your fathers; you shall be my people, and I will be your God.

There is an interesting challenge for us in this reading. There are those of us who work hard at our faith, and grow in small, purposeful steps, and there are those who are knocked off of their horses and change their lives in an instant. There are people who are faithful, yet live difficult lives, and people who are completely unfaithful and live in prosperity. Why would God allow that?

In previous readings, the Israelites have repented and desire a return to their God and their lives. However, this group hasn't done that at all. Still, God will bring them back and give them a little extra help. They will be cleansed and refreshed. They will listen and be reunited. Through this mercy, the world will see the power of God, and maybe they can be drawn just a little bit closer.

Food for Thought

1. Has your faith grown in small, hard-fought steps or developed in sudden bursts?

2. Do you think the sudden, seemingly undeserved bursts help build belief in God? Why or why not?

Responsorial Psalm *Psalm 42:3, 5; 43:3, 4*

In his letter to the Romans, Paul talks about Jesus' death in a remarkable parallel to the seventh reading that we have just heard. "For Christ, while we were still helpless, yet died at the appointed time for the ungodly. Indeed, only with difficulty does on die for a just person, though perhaps for a good person one might even find courage to die. But God proves his love for us in that while we were still sinners Christ died for us." (Romans 5:6-8)

    Jesus died for the very ones who killed Him. He dies for us, even when we deny Him. None of us is worthy, yet Jesus gave His life anyway. As we finish our Old Testament readings, our longing for Easter grows stronger and stronger. We have been waiting since the beginning of Lent. Feel this moment as we sing the next Psalm.

- ***Psalm 42:3, 5; 43:3, 4*** [1]

    R. (42:2) Like a deer that longs for running streams, my soul longs for you, my God.

    Athirst is my soul for God, the living God.
    When shall I go and behold the face of God?

    R. Like a deer that longs for running streams, my soul longs for you, my God.

    I went with the throng
    and led them in procession to the house of God,
    Amid loud cries of joy and thanksgiving,
    with the multitude keeping festival.

    R. Like a deer that longs for running streams, my soul longs for you, my God.

    Send forth your light and your fidelity;
    they shall lead me on
    And bring me to your holy mountain,
    to your dwelling-place.

    R. Like a deer that longs for running streams, my soul longs for you, my God.

    Then will I go in to the altar of God,
    the God of my gladness and joy;
    then will I give you thanks upon the harp,
    O God, my God!

    R. Like a deer that longs for running streams, my soul longs for you, my God.

As we approach the end of the Old Testament readings, we are filled with a longing for God. Each of these readings promises that God will come to us. Each one tells us of a closeness that is beyond anything we have ever imagined. Do you feel it? Are you ready?

---

[1] ALTERNATE READING IS FOUND IN APPENDIX A

Food for Thought

1. Have you ever had a longing for God in your soul? Do you have it now?

2. How would you respond if God filled you with His presence right now? If He answered the prayer to send forth His light and fidelity, what would you do?

3. Do you think God answers those kinds of prayers? How?

Gloria

As the notes from the Psalm fade away, we enter into my favorite part of Holy Saturday. As we transition to the New Testament, the altar candles are lit, the lights are turned on if they've been kept off, the bells ring wildly and continuously, and we sing out with the angels in voices that fill the church, "Glory to God in the highest, and on earth, peace."

The Light has come into the world, and the darkness that descended on Good Friday is suddenly dispelled. We have crossed into a new creation, and all that was hidden in the Old Testament is now revealed in Jesus Christ. Everything about it is glorious.

Epistle (Eighth Reading) *Romans 6:3-11*

Our first reading from the New Testament reminds us how we personally enter into the mystery of Jesus' death and resurrection. Our lives will not be problem-free just because we follow Christ, no matter how faithful we are, and we will all experience suffering. However, our faith helps us to remember that through great suffering comes great blessing. It is no different for us in our lives today.

- *Romans 6:3-11*

    Brothers and sisters:

    Are you unaware that we who were baptized into Christ Jesus were baptized into his death? We were indeed buried with him through baptism into death, so that, just as Christ was raised from the dead by the glory of the Father, we too might live in newness of life.

    For if we have grown into union with him through a death like his, we shall also be united with him in the resurrection. We know that our old self was crucified with him, so that our sinful body might be done away with, that we might no longer be in slavery to sin. For a dead person has been absolved from sin. If, then, we have died with Christ, we believe that we shall also live with him. We know that Christ, raised from the dead, dies no more; death no longer has power over him. As to his death, he died to sin once and for all; as to his life, he lives for God. Consequently, you too must think of yourselves as being dead to sin and living for God in Christ Jesus.

As we approach the end of the story of our salvation being told today, the light and hope that fill the readings are astounding. We have come through days of suffering and pain, betrayal and abandonment. All is brought to fulfillment now, and joy has returned. We are freed from the bondage of slavery to sin; we have only to claim it. We can rise from the dead with Jesus. Now is the time.

Food for Thought

1. The temptation to sin can be very enticing. Have you found a time when your faith has allowed you to turn away from temptation?

2. How has your faith brought you life?

Responsorial Psalm
Psalm 118:1-2, 16-17, 22-23

In this final Psalm, we sing the "Alleluia" that has been missing for all of Lent. Most of the time, we sing it with a small verse related to the Gospel. This time, we add several verses to our proclamation. See how the meaning changes with the events of the last several days.

- *Psalm 118:1-2, 16-17, 22-23*

    R. Alleluia, alleluia, alleluia.

    Give thanks to the LORD, for he is good,
    for his mercy endures forever.
    Let the house of Israel say,
    "His mercy endures forever."

    R. Alleluia, alleluia, alleluia.

    The right hand of the LORD has struck with power;
    the right hand of the LORD is exalted.
    I shall not die, but live,
    and declare the works of the LORD.

    R. Alleluia, alleluia, alleluia.

    The stone which the builders rejected
    has become the cornerstone.
    By the LORD has this been done;
    it is wonderful in our eyes.

    R. Alleluia, alleluia, alleluia.

These verses were written many hundreds of years before Jesus died, yet they tell of the work that was done through Him. Jesus, who we thought was dead, is alive. He was rejected, but has become the very base or cornerstone of our faith. The Lord has done this. It is good.

Food for Thought

1. Does it make a difference to you that the words of Psalm 118 were written long before Jesus died?

2. After going through Holy Week, what meaning do you find in the words of Psalm 118 as you sing them?

Gospel *Matthew 28:1-10*

As I said at the beginning of this book – for most of us, the story of Easter has become just that: a story. As we read the Gospel account of the discovery of the empty tomb, I want you to look at the story with fresh eyes. Imagine that you are one of the women who came to the tomb. You have no expectation other than to prepare the body for burial. Instead, as you arrive, an empty tomb and an angel greet you. You are told to tell the other followers of Christ. Do you run? Do you stand in disbelief? How do you explain it? What could you possibly say? These women had no idea that the Resurrection was coming. Imagine being in their shoes.

Imagine you are one of the women at the tomb. How do you explain it? What could you possibly say?

- *Matthew 28:1-10*[1]

> After the sabbath, as the first day of the week was dawning, Mary Magdalene and the other Mary came to see the tomb. And behold, there was a great earthquake; for an angel of the Lord descended from heaven, approached, rolled back the stone, and sat upon it. His appearance was like lightning and his clothing was white as snow. The guards were shaken with fear of him and became like dead men. Then the angel said to the women in reply, "Do not be afraid! I know that you are seeking Jesus the crucified. He is not here, for he has been raised just as he said. Come and see the place where he lay. Then go quickly and tell his disciples, 'He has been raised from the dead, and he is going before you to Galilee; there you will see him.' Behold, I have told you." Then they went away quickly from the tomb, fearful yet overjoyed, and ran to announce this to his disciples. And behold, Jesus met them on their way and greeted them. They approached, embraced his feet, and did him homage. Then Jesus said to them, "Do not be afraid. Go tell my brothers to go to Galilee, and there they will see me."

I have no idea how I would react at this moment. An earthquake has opened the tomb, and the guards are unconscious on the ground before me, so they're out. This angel with an appearance like lightning tells me not to be afraid. I know that statement wouldn't make me feel much better. But then I would see that the tomb was empty, and on my way back, I would see Jesus standing alive in front of me. I'm pretty sure I would collapse to my feet in a puddle of tears, relief, and questions. And again, I would hear, "Do not be afraid."

---

[1] READINGS FOR YEARS B AND C ARE FOUND IN APPENDIX A

Food for Thought

1. The women are "fearful yet overjoyed" as they hear that Jesus has been raised from the dead. How would you have responded as you approached the empty tomb?

2. The first thing that the women do is run to tell the others what they saw. When you have an experience of God, whom do you tell about it?

3. Why is it important to tell others about our experiences?

As we complete the Liturgy of the Word, this final reading brings us to the pinnacle of our faith. Without the Resurrection, Jesus was nothing more than another prophet, and a very poor one at that. With the Resurrection, everything changes. The Holy of Holies is opened, the power of death is overcome, and God's love has been proven to go well beyond this life that we know. At this point in the story, however, none of this is clear. All that is clear is that Jesus is no longer dead, and the Messiah that they thought they had in Him has returned. There is much more for the disciples to understand.

Our own faith is so similar. We can discover truths that we didn't understand before, and still have much to learn. We can make great leaps in our faith and knowledge, and still have no concept of what God will do with it. Fortunately for us, we have a God who is patient and who never gives up on us. Easter doesn't end here. It is just beginning.

Rites of Initiation

Once the Liturgy of the Word is complete, we begin the Rites of Initiation and welcome new converts into the Church. The three rites celebrated tonight are Baptism, Confirmation, and First Communion. There have been many books dedicated to explaining the meaning and significance of each of these sacraments. For our purposes today, I will give a brief overview of each one.[1]

Most Catholics receive Baptism, Confirmation, and their First Communion at different times in their lives, and we don't often realize that they are intimately connected. Tonight, however, we see that each one celebrates a unique gift and grace that Jesus gives us in the Catholic Church.

---

[1] FOR A DETAILED LOOK AT EACH OF THESE SACRAMENTS REFER TO THE CATECHISM OF THE CATHOLIC CHURCH. BAPTISM: PARAGRAPHS 1213-1284; CONFIRMATION: PARAGRAPHS 1285-1321; EUCHARIST: PARAGRAPHS 1322-1419

Each [sacrament] celebrates a unique gift and grace that Jesus gives us in the Catholic Church

Baptism

The Baptismal Liturgy begins with a Litany of the Saints, where we ask for mercy and deliverance from God, and for prayers from the Saints. Specifically, we ask for the prayers of the baptismal and confirmation Saints of the people entering the Catholic Church at this Mass. The blessing of the baptismal water, and a profession of faith from those about to be baptized follow this Litany. For the blessing of the water, the priest dips the Paschal candle into the water three times praying that God send the Holy Spirit to bless the water. Just as Jesus entered the waters of the Jordan and transformed them into the waters of baptism with the Holy Spirit, this candle representing Christ and the words of blessing transform the water into Holy water. After professing their faith and belief in Jesus Christ and His Church, the candidates are ready to enter into a new life in Christ.

The people receiving Baptism tonight are immersed or have water poured over their heads three times – in the name of the Father, the Son, and the Holy Spirit.

> *"Amen, amen, I say to you, no one can enter the kingdom of God without being born of water and Spirit." (John 3:5)*

HOLY WATER

After the Holy Saturday liturgy is completed, the Holy Water fonts will be filled with the waters of baptism used today. We are reminded of our own baptisms every time we bless ourselves in the name of the Father, the Son, and of the Holy Spirit.

In this way, they are reborn into a life in Christ, and become members of the family of God. Once they are baptized, they are given a new, white garment to symbolize their being washed clean of sin and being given a new life in Christ. They are given a candle, lit from the Paschal candle, to remind them of the Light of Christ in their lives, and they are anointed with Holy Chrism as a sign of the outpouring of the Holy Spirit.

As the candidates enter into our community, we are reminded that we are part of this family, ready to welcome them into the fold. As a congregation, we renew our own baptismal promises, we are sprinkled with Holy water, and we light our candles once more from the light of the Paschal candle. We are reminded of our own baptism and of our lives as children of God.

Confirmation

The Baptismal Rite is immediately followed by Confirmation. Most people think that the purpose of Confirmation is to claim your faith as your own, or to become an adult member in the Church. In a way, this is true. This sacrament confirms and completes the process that began in baptism. However, Confirmation is much more than just a statement of faith.

In the Bible, Jesus promises the Apostles that He will send them an Advocate to be with them always.[1] The apostles had already proclaimed their faith in Jesus. This was going to be something altogether different.[1] After the Holy Spirit descends upon the disciples at Pentecost, they leave from their hiding place behind closed doors. Instead, they go out to the world, proclaiming Christ crucified and risen to anyone who will listen, unafraid of any punishment or consequence that may come.

Confirmation deepens the effect of baptismal grace and increases the gifts of the Holy Spirit in those who receive it. This descent of the Holy Spirit gives power that is beyond that given by baptism. It is this power that we claim tonight. It is this Spirit that we call down and ask to enkindle the hearts of the faithful.

---

[1] JOHN 14:16-17

[2] THE UNDERSTANDING OF BAPTISM AND CONFIRMATION AS SEPARATE EVENTS CAN ALSO BE FOUND IN ACTS 8:14-17; 9:10-19; AND 10:44-48. THE HOLY SPIRIT IS CONFERRED EACH TIME BY THE LAYING ON OF HANDS.

The priest confers the sacrament of Confirmation by anointing each person with the Oil of Chrism and laying hands on their foreheads saying, "Be sealed with the gift of the Holy Spirit." He then offers them a sign of peace, indicating communion with all of the faithful.

First Holy Communion

Finally, everyone at Mass participates in the Liturgy of the Eucharist. For the people entering the Church, this is the first time they have been allowed to participate fully and receive Holy Communion. For many of them, the longing for this moment has been immense. As full members of the Catholic Church, they are now invited to participate in the meal that was offered to us in the Holy Thursday service. We approach the altar together, united in our faith, consuming the victim whose life has been offered for us, and receiving the grace of the Resurrection given to us on this most holy of nights.

Concluding Rite

Finally, we are dismissed. The Mass that began on Thursday, and continued through Friday, comes to its climax and conclusion tonight. Christ has died, Christ is Risen, Christ will come again. We are told to go in peace. Thanks be to God.

Mass Moments

Holy Saturday is a long and involved Mass. Look over this chapter and think about the things you want to look for, remember, or appreciate as you attend Mass on Holy Saturday. Write them down on the pages in the back.

CHAPTER 6

Easter Sunday: Discovery of a New World

It was midnight after the Holy Saturday Mass, and I was standing at a reception for the people whom had just received the sacraments of baptism, confirmation, and first Communion. It was a joyful night, and one that was special for our family because we were celebrating for a good friend. As I approached my friend's husband to congratulate him, he was shaking his head in disbelief. "Can you believe she wants to go again tomorrow?" He was incredulous. They had just sat through three hours of church, the next Mass was only hours away, and she was ready to go again. "She's had her first Communion, and she can't wait to go get her second. She is asking me how I could waste this chance to go to Easter Mass and celebrate." Of course, they went.

Entry

After going through all of the days of Holy Week, it is hard to imagine leaving church on Palm Sunday and not returning until Easter morning. So much has happened in the days in between. There has already been such joy and celebration, and today is just the continuation.

Today the priests wear white vestments, and we enter with joyful song, the church filled with flowers, light, and beauty. For some, this Mass is held at dawn as the sun is rising, beautifully symbolizing the rising of the Son of God from the dead. It is a glorious moment, and everything about this Mass reflects the joy in it.

First Reading *Acts 10:34a, 37-43*

Like we did on Palm Sunday, we start today a little out of order. The event in this first reading happens long after Jesus' resurrection. Peter has been out preaching and spreading the word about what has happened and who Jesus is, and here he proclaims the good news to the family of Cornelius, a Roman centurion and Gentile.

It's a good summary for us as we prepare to enter the tomb. We already know what we are about to see. We know what has happened. How would you tell others who had no idea? Imagine hearing it yourself for the first time.

> *If we can believe, if we can truly accept that Jesus died for our sins, then we can receive the payment that was made and the grace that was given.*

■ *Acts 10:34a, 37-43*

Peter proceeded to speak and said: "You know what has happened all over Judea, beginning in Galilee after the baptism that John preached, how God anointed Jesus of Nazareth with the Holy Spirit and power. He went about doing good and healing all those oppressed by the devil, for God was with him. We are witnesses of all that he did both in the country of the Jews and in Jerusalem. They put him to death by hanging him on a tree. This man God raised on the third day and granted that he be visible, not to all the people, but to us, the witnesses chosen by God in advance, who ate and drank with him after he rose from the dead. He commissioned us to preach to the people and testify that he is the one appointed by God as judge of the living and the dead. To him all the prophets bear witness, that everyone who believes in him will receive forgiveness of sins through his name."

DETAILS, DETAILS

It is interesting to me that Peter mentions eating and drinking with Jesus. If you had witnessed the resurrected Jesus, how would you possibly explain what had happened to anyone who wasn't there? Today, even if you are not a Christian, you have at least heard of the concept. In Peter's time, someone rising from the dead was unheard of. Peter had to explain that this was not some hallucination, ghost, or dream. This was not an explanation for a body that had disappeared. It was real, it was physical, and it was crucial to the understanding of what Jesus' death had done.

Having paid the price for sin, Jesus offers that payment for anyone who believes in Him. It's funny how that can be such a hard thing to accept. My husband was an atheist when I married him, and one of the things that bothered him was that you had to believe in Jesus in order to be "saved." To him, it was a complete power trip, and he wanted nothing to do with it. If he was a good person, trying to do the right thing, that should be enough. It turns out that this understanding, like so many that he had, was completely backwards. Jesus doesn't need us to believe in Him so that He feels valued or because He needs us to see His sacrifice as important. He needs us to believe that what He did was for us. That's all. If we can believe, if we can truly accept that Jesus died for our sins, then we can receive the payment that was made and the grace that was given.

It's like going to the payment window at a drive-through restaurant. If we are told that the person in front of us paid for our meal, we can believe that information, receive the food, and eat without paying the cost. If we refuse to believe it, no matter how insistent the cashier may be, we will leave our money, paying the cost ourselves, and refuse the gift that has been offered to us. After all, it is our choice. The person paying did so without knowing if the gift would be accepted or not. It was given freely and generously. All we need to do is believe and the gift is ours.

> **NEW TESTAMENT ONLY**
>
> For the next several weeks, there will be no Old Testament reading during the celebration of the Mass. Instead, we will go through the Acts of the Apostles and watch the Church grow from a group of frightened people in a locked room to one that is recognized and spreading throughout the world. Once the fifty-day Easter season is over, we will return to the standard format of the first reading on Sunday coming from the Old Testament.

Food for Thought

1. What are some of the things that make it hard for you to believe in Jesus?

2. What are some of the things you find important to tell others about who Jesus is? Why?

Responsorial Psalm ■ *Psalm 118:1-2, 16-17, 22-23*

Can you even begin to imagine the state of Jesus' followers when they realized that Jesus had risen from the dead? If you have ever lost someone close to you, you know that there is a part of you that would do almost anything to have that person back, even for a moment. Imagine reading or reciting this Psalm in the view of the empty tomb, knowing that Jesus was alive. These words, written so long before this moment, should be sung from the mountaintops.

- *Psalm 118:1-2, 16-17, 22-23*

   **R. (24) This is the day the Lord has made;
   let us rejoice and be glad. or R. Alleluia.**

   Give thanks to the LORD, for he is good,
      for his mercy endures forever.
   Let the house of Israel say,
      "His mercy endures forever."

   **R. (24) This is the day the Lord has made;
   let us rejoice and be glad. or R. Alleluia.**

   "The right hand of the LORD has struck with power;
      the right hand of the LORD is exalted.
   I shall not die, but live,
      and declare the works of the LORD."

   **R. (24) This is the day the Lord has made;
   let us rejoice and be glad. or R. Alleluia.**

   The stone which the builders rejected
      has become the cornerstone.
   By the LORD has this been done;
      it is wonderful in our eyes.

   **R. (24) This is the day the Lord has made;
   let us rejoice and be glad. or R. Alleluia.**

This Psalm is a striking contrast to Psalm 22. Instead of giving thanks in the midst of suffering and persecution, this Psalm sings of the glory and triumph of God. It is the difference between Good Friday and Easter. We all have our moments of suffering and loss. We all have our moments when God allows us to become aware of our shortcomings and failures. We can be thankful and hopeful for the work of God within it, but we must never stop there. We place our sins and our sorrows on the Cross, and we leave them to look toward the Resurrection. We are called to be an Easter people, knowing that "His mercy endures forever." Let us rejoice and be glad.

Food for Thought

1. When is the last time you have rejoiced in a day that the Lord has made?

2. What would help you to rejoice more often?

Second Reading *Colossians 3:1-4*

As we continue our readings for Easter Sunday, we are given instructions on how to live this new life we have been given. This will continue in the weeks following Easter. We can make it so complicated, but these few verses help us to remember that the reality is really pretty simple.

- *Colossians 3:1-4*

    Brothers and sisters:

    If then you were raised with Christ, seek what is above, where Christ is seated at the right hand of God. Think of what is above, not of what is on earth. For you have died, and your life is hidden with Christ in God. When Christ your life appears, then you too will appear with him in glory.

These words are so simple, yet they can be incredibly difficult to live out every day. It is tempting to leave our faith at the door when we leave the church each week, but our call is to carry it with us always. We are to seek what is above and think of what is above. If we live our lives in the context of heaven, it will be a radically different way of living than before. If we live this way, then we try to see everyone with the eyes of Jesus. We attempt to love everyone with the heart of God. We will live our calling with the power of the Holy Spirit. Such a simple concept, yet such a drastic difference.

Food for Thought

1. How do you think your life will be different after this Easter?

2. Should your life be different? Why or why not?

Easter Sequence

Before the Gospel, the Easter Sequence will be read or sung. It is an ancient poem that tells us the story of the Resurrection and is a mandatory part of the Easter Sunday Mass. It sets the stage for what we are about to hear, and brings us into the story just a little bit more.

Christians, to the Paschal Victim
Offer your thankful praises!
A Lamb the sheep redeems;
Christ, who only is sinless,
Reconciles sinners to the Father.
Death and life have contended in that combat stupendous:
The Prince of life, who died, reigns immortal.
Speak, Mary, declaring
What you saw, wayfaring.
"The tomb of Christ, who is living,
The glory of Jesus' resurrection;
bright angels attesting,
The shroud and napkin resting.
Yes, Christ my hope is arisen;
to Galilee he goes before you."
Christ indeed from death is risen, our new life obtaining.
Have mercy, victor King, ever reigning!
Amen. Alleluia.

Gospel

John 20:1-9

I find this reading very interesting. We are so used to the story that the unusual aspects of it may not stand out to us. This recounting of the discovery of the empty tomb was told to all who would listen, as part of the story of the salvation of the risen Christ. Pay attention to how John tells the tale.

- *John 20:1-9* [1]

    On the first day of the week, Mary of Magdala came to the tomb early in the morning, while it was still dark, and saw the stone removed from the tomb. So she ran and went to Simon Peter and to the other disciple whom Jesus loved, and told them, "They have taken the Lord from the tomb, and we don't know where they put him." So Peter and the other disciple went out and came to the tomb. They both ran, but the other disciple ran faster than Peter and arrived at the tomb first; he bent down and saw the burial cloths there, but did not go in. When Simon Peter arrived after him, he went into the tomb and saw the burial cloths there, and the cloth that had covered his head, not with the burial cloths but rolled up in a separate place. Then the other disciple also went in, the one who had arrived at the tomb first, and he saw and believed. For they did not yet understand the Scripture that he had to rise from the dead.

Now, if you were telling the story of your involvement in a major event, you might tell your friends about the things you did wrong or the ways that you misinterpreted what was going on, but you would never share that part of the story as a part of your sales pitch to the rest of the world. However, we often see the disciples of Jesus in an unflattering light. This most significant of moments is no exception.

---

[1] ALTERNATE READING IS FOUND IN APPENDIX A

They don't show that power by building themselves up beyond what they really are. They lay everything bare to show that the power within them is not their own, but truly the power of God.

Surprisingly, a woman, Mary Magadala is the first one to the tomb, not one of the Apostles. Not only that, she's a woman who used to have seven demons – not quite the highest level of society in this one. Then, they admit that Mary of Magdala has no idea what happened. The Gospels mention several times when Jesus predicts his own death and resurrection, and even as it happens, they miss it. Shortly afterward, the two disciples run to the tomb. One is too frightened even to enter, and only goes in after Peter shows up. Finally, they believe that Jesus has risen, but admit that they still do not understand what is going on. If they are trying to set themselves up as experts in their field, none of this is helping their case.

This is one of the reasons that the Gospels are given such credibility. So often we read the Bible as high literature, giving it an aura that covers what we are reading with a holy glow. Without denying that this is the Word of God, it is helpful to remove that glow and look to see the human side of the writers. Imagine that you had been a part of this incredible event. How would you explain it to people? How could you possibly tell the story? The best way is to tell it the way that it happened.

Read these Scriptures from the perspective of an uneducated fisherman, a sinful tax collector, or some other marginalized, disregarded member of society. See how they try to describe what has happened, and how they lay everything bare to show that the power within them is not their own, but is truly the power of God. They don't show that power by building themselves up beyond what they really are. They do it by showing their weaknesses and their frailties, their failings and their missteps.

The Gospel writers show us that these events were difficult and confusing for those who were closest to it. We will see in the weeks ahead that it is only by the power of the Holy Spirit that the understanding and wisdom comes to them. We can rest in knowing we are offered the same.

Food for Thought

1. What kinds of stories help increase your faith?

2. Do you find it hard to share times when you have failed or been weak? Why or why not?

3. How have you shared your own faith with others? What stories do you tell?

Conclusion

How do you recover from this? After writing about these days of Holy Week, I hardly know what to say as we come to the end of Mass on this Easter Sunday. I stand in shock as I find the empty tomb. The apostles are still waiting to see Jesus, and so are we.

If we are experiencing this as it is presented at each Mass, then we could easily be in one of two places. We could see the empty tomb as proof that Jesus has risen from the dead, or we could wonder what these things could mean. Either way, we could ask: Is Jesus back, or is He just gone? What is really happening? Where do we go from here?

Fortunately, the Easter season doesn't end on Easter Sunday; it is just beginning. The world as we know it has completely changed. We have fifty days to understand what we have just gone through. We have weeks to adjust to our new normal. I hope that what you have read has blessed you and that you have participated in the days leading up to Easter in ways that you never have before. I pray that your experience of the risen Jesus has only just begun to transform your life.

We are sent out from this final Mass of Holy Week with a blessing and a command. As you leave on Easter Sunday, may you go forth and proclaim the Good News.

Mass Moments

Look over this chapter and think about the things you want to look for, remember, or appreciate as you attend Mass on Easter Sunday. Write them down on the pages in the back.

APPENDIX A

Year B and C Readings

Palm Sunday Readings

Palm Sunday Entrance Gospel:

Year B:
Mark 11:1-10 or John 12:12-16

■ *Mark 11:1-10*

> When Jesus and his disciples drew near to Jerusalem, to Bethphage and Bethany at the Mount of Olives, he sent two of his disciples and said to them, "Go into the village opposite you, and immediately on entering it, you will find a cold tethered on which no one has ever sat. Untie it and bring it here. If anyone should say to you, 'Why are you doing this?' reply, 'The Master has need of it and will send it back here at once.'" So they went off and found a colt tethered at a gate outside on the street, and they untied it. Some of the bystanders said to them, "What are you doing, untying the colt?" They answered them just as Jesus had told them to, and they permitted them to do it. So they brought the colt to Jesus and put their cloaks over it. And he sat on it. Many people spread their cloaks on the road, and others spread leafy branches that they had cut from the fields. Those preceding him as well as those following kept crying out:
>
> "Hosanna!
>   Blessed is he who comes in the name of the Lord!
>   Blessed is the kingdom of our father David that is to come!
> Hosanna in the highest!"

■ *John 12:12-16*

> When the great crowd that had come to the feast heard that Jesus was coming to Jerusalem, they took palm branches and went out to meet him, and cried out:

> "Hosanna!
> Blessed is he who comes in the name of the Lord,
>   the king of Israel."

> Jesus found an ass and sat upon it, as it is written:
>   Fear no more, O daughter Zion:
>   see, you king comes, seated upon an ass's colt.

> His disciples did not understand this at first, but when Jesus had been glorified they remembered that these things were written about him and that they had done this for him.

Year C:
- **Luke 19:28-40**

> (Notice the Pharisees complaining about Jesus' entry. As the celebration continues, we can see that dissent is festering. All is not well.)

> Jesus proceeded on his journey up to Jerusalem. As he drew near to Bethphage and Bethany at the place called the Mount of Olives, he sent two of his disciples. He said, "Go into the village opposite you, and as you enter it you will find a colt tethered on which no one has ever sat. Untie it and bring it here. And if anyone should ask you, 'Why are you untying it?' you will answer, 'The Master has need of it.'" So those who had been sent went off and found everything just as he had told them. And as they were untying the colt, its owners said to them, "Why are you untying this colt?" They answered, "The Master has need of it." So they brought it to Jesus, threw their cloaks over the colt, and helped Jesus to mount. As he rode along, the people were spreading their cloaks on the road; and now as he was approaching the slope of the Mount of Olives, the whole multitude of his disciples began to praise God aloud with joy for all the mighty deeds they had seen. They proclaimed:

> "Blessed is the king who comes
>   in the name of the Lord.

> *Peace in heaven*
>> *and glory in the highest."*
>
> *Some of the Pharisees in the crowd said to him, "Teacher, rebuke your disciples." He said in reply, "I tell you, if they keep silent, the stones will cry out!"*

Palm Sunday Gospel:
Year B:
- *Mark 14:1-15:47 (short version Mark 15:1-39)*

> *The Passover and the Feast of Unleavened Bread were to take place in two days' time. So the chief priests and the scribes were seeking a way to arrest him by treachery and put him to death. They said, "Not during the festival, for fear that there may be a riot among the people."*
>
> *When he was in Bethany reclining at table in the house of Simon the leper, a woman came with an alabaster jar of perfumed oil, costly genuine spikenard. She broke the alabaster jar and poured it on his head. There were some who were indignant. "Why has there been this waste of perfumed oil? It could have been sold for more than three hundred days' wages and the money given to the poor." They were infuriated with her. Jesus said, "Let her alone. Why do you make trouble for her? She has done a good thing for me. The poor you will always have with you, and whenever you wish you can do good to them, but you will not always have me. She has done what she could. She has anticipated anointing my body for burial. Amen, I say to you, wherever the gospel is proclaimed to the whole world, what she has done will be told in memory of her."*
>
> *Then Judas Iscariot, one of the Twelve, went off to the chief priests to hand him over to them. When they heard him they were pleased and promised to pay him money. Then he looked for an opportunity to hand him over.*
>
> *On the first day of the Feast of Unleavened Bread, when they sacrificed the Passover lamb, his disciples said to him, "Where do you want us to go and prepare for you to eat the Passover?" He sent two of his*

disciples and said to them, "Go into the city and a man will meet you, carrying a jar of water. Follow him. Wherever he enters, say to the master of the house, 'The Teacher says, "Where is my guest room where I may eat the Passover with my disciples?"' Then he will show you a large upper room furnished and ready. Make the preparations for us there." The disciples then went off, entered the city, and found it just as he had told them; and they prepared the Passover.

When it was evening, he came with the Twelve. And as they reclined at table and were eating, Jesus said, "Amen, I say to you, one of you will betray me, one who is eating with me." They began to be distressed and to say to him, one by one, "Surely it is not I?" He said to them, "One of the Twelve, the one who dips with me into the dish. For the Son of Man indeed goes, as it is written of him, but woe to that man by whom the Son of Man is betrayed. It would be better for that man if he had never been born."

While they were eating, he took bread, said the blessing, broke it, and gave it to them, and said, "Take it; this is my body." Then he took a cup, gave thanks, and gave it to them, and they all drank from it. He said to them, "This is my blood of the covenant, which will be shed for many. Amen, I say to you, I shall not drink again the fruit of the vine until the day when I drink it new in the kingdom of God." Then, after singing a hymn, they went out to the Mount of Olives.

Then Jesus said to them, "All of you will have your faith shaken, for it is written:

    I will strike the shepherd,
        and the sheep will be dispersed.

But after I have been raised up, I shall go before you to Galilee." Peter said to him, "Even though all should have their faith shaken, mine will not be." Then Jesus said to him, "Amen, I say to you, this very night before the cock crows twice you will deny me three times." But he vehemently replied, "Even though I should have to die with you, I will not deny you." And they all spoke similarly.

Then they came to a place named Gethsemane, and he said to his disciples, "Sit here while I pray." He took with him Peter, James, and

John, and began to be troubled and distressed. Then he said to them, "My soul is sorrowful even to death. Remain here and keep watch." He advanced a little and fell to the ground and prayed that if it were possible the hour might pass by him; he said, "Abba, Father, all things are possible to you. Take this cup away from me, but not what I will but what you will." When he returned he found them asleep. He said to Peter, "Simon, are you asleep? Could you not keep watch for one hour? Watch and pray that you may not undergo the test. The spirit is willing but the flesh is weak." Withdrawing again, he prayed, saying the same thing. Then he returned once more and found them asleep, for they could not keep their eyes open and did not know what to answer him. He returned a third time and said to them, "Are you still sleeping and taking your rest? It is enough. The hour has come. Behold, the Son of Man is to be handed over to sinners. Get up, let us go. See, my betrayer is at hand."

Then, while he was still speaking, Judas, one of the Twelve, arrived, accompanied by a crowd with swords and clubs who had come from the chief priests, the scribes, and the elders. His betrayer had arranged a signal with them, saying, "The man I shall kiss is the one; arrest him and lead him away securely." He came and immediately went over to him and said, "Rabbi." And he kissed him. At this they laid hands on him and arrested him. One of the bystanders drew his sword, struck the high priest's servant, and cut off his ear. Jesus said to them in reply, "Have you come out as against a robber, with swords and clubs, to seize me? Day after day I was with you teaching in the temple area, yet you did not arrest me; but that the Scriptures may be fulfilled." And they all left him and fled. Now a young man followed him wearing nothing but a linen cloth about his body. They seized him, but he left the cloth behind and ran off naked.

They led Jesus away to the high priest, and all the chief priests and the elders and the scribes came together. Peter followed him at a distance into the high priest's courtyard and was seated with the guards, warming himself at the fire. The chief priests and the entire Sanhedrin kept trying to obtain testimony against Jesus in order to put him to death, but they found none. Many gave false witness against him, but their testimony did not agree. Some took the stand and testified falsely against him, alleging, "We heard him say, 'I will destroy this temple made with hands and within three days I will build another not made with hands.'" Even so their testimony did not agree. The high priest rose before the assembly and questioned Jesus, saying, "Have you no answer? What are these men testifying against you?" But he was silent and answered nothing. Again the high priest asked him and said to him, "Are you the Christ, the son of the Blessed One?" Then Jesus answered, "I am;

> *and 'you will see the Son of Man*
> > *seated at the right hand of the Power*
> > *and coming with the clouds of heaven.'"*

At that the high priest tore his garments and said, "What further need have we of witnesses? You have heard the blasphemy. What do you think?" They all condemned him as deserving to die. Some began to spit on him. They blindfolded him and struck him and said to him, "Prophesy!" And the guards greeted him with blows.

While Peter was below in the courtyard, one of the high priest's maids came along. Seeing Peter warming himself, she looked intently at him and said, "You too were with the Nazarene, Jesus." But he denied it saying, "I neither know nor understand what you are talking about." So he went out into the outer court. Then the cock crowed. The maid saw him and began again to say to the bystanders, "This man is one of them." Once again he denied it. A little later the bystanders said to Peter once more, "Surely you are one of them; for you too are a Galilean." He began to curse and to swear, "I do not know this man about whom you are talking." And immediately a cock crowed a second time. Then Peter remembered the word that Jesus had said to him, "Before the cock crows twice you will deny me three times." He broke down and wept.

As soon as morning came, the chief priests with the elders and the scribes, that is, the whole Sanhedrin held a council. They bound Jesus, led him away, and handed him over to Pilate. Pilate questioned him, "Are you the king of the Jews?" He said to him in reply, "You say so." The chief priests accused him of many things. Again Pilate questioned him,

"Have you no answer? See how many things they accuse you of." Jesus gave him no further answer, so that Pilate was amazed.

Now on the occasion of the feast he used to release to them one prisoner whom they requested. A man called Barabbas was then in prison along with the rebels who had committed murder in a rebellion. The crowd came forward and began to ask him to do for them as he was accustomed. Pilate answered, "Do you want me to release to you the king of the Jews?" For he knew that it was out of envy that the chief priests had handed him over. But the chief priests stirred up the crowd to have him release Barabbas for them instead. Pilate again said to them in reply, "Then what do you want me to do with the man you call the king of the Jews?" They shouted again, "Crucify him." Pilate said to them, "Why? What evil has he done?" They only shouted the louder, "Crucify him." So Pilate, wishing to satisfy the crowd, released Barabbas to them and, after he had Jesus scourged, handed him over to be crucified.

The soldiers led him away inside the palace, that is, the praetorium, and assembled the whole cohort. They clothed him in purple and, weaving a crown of thorns, placed it on him. They began to salute him with, "Hail, King of the Jews!" and kept striking his head with a reed and spitting upon him. They knelt before him in homage. And when they had mocked him, they stripped him of the purple cloak, dressed him in his own clothes, and led him out to crucify him.

They pressed into service a passer-by, Simon, a Cyrenian, who was coming in from the country, the father of Alexander and Rufus, to carry his cross.

They brought him to the place of Golgotha — which is translated Place of the Skull —. They gave him wine drugged with myrrh, but he did not take it. Then they crucified him and divided his garments by casting lots for them to see what each should take. It was nine o'clock in the morning when they crucified him. The inscription of the charge against him read, "The King of the Jews." With him they crucified two revolutionaries, one on his right and one on his left. Those passing by reviled him, shaking their heads and saying, "Aha! You who would destroy the temple and rebuild it in three days, save yourself by coming down from the cross." Likewise the chief priests, with the scribes, mocked him among themselves and said, "He saved others; he cannot save himself. Let the Christ, the King of Israel, come down now from the cross that we may see and believe." Those who were crucified with him also kept abusing him.

At noon darkness came over the whole land until three in the afternoon. And at three o'clock Jesus cried out in a loud voice, "Eloi, Eloi, lema sabachthani?" which is translated, "My God, my God, why have you forsaken me?" Some of the bystanders who heard it said, "Look, he is calling Elijah." One of them ran, soaked a sponge with wine, put it on a reed and gave it to him to drink saying, "Wait, let us see if Elijah comes to take him down." Jesus gave a loud cry and breathed his last.

(Here all kneel and pause for a short time)

The veil of the sanctuary was torn in two from top to bottom. When the centurion who stood facing him saw how he breathed his last he said, "Truly this man was the Son of God!" There were also women looking on from a distance. Among them were Mary Magdalene, Mary the mother of the younger James and of Joses, and Salome. These women had followed him when he was in Galilee and ministered to him. There were also many other women who had come up with him to Jerusalem.

When it was already evening, since it was the day of preparation, the day before the sabbath, Joseph of Arimathea, a distinguished member of the council, who was himself awaiting the kingdom of God, came and courageously went to Pilate and asked for the body of Jesus. Pilate was amazed that he was already dead. He summoned the centurion and asked him if Jesus had already died. And when he learned of it from the centurion, he gave the body to Joseph. Having bought a linen cloth, he took him down, wrapped him in the linen cloth, and laid him in a tomb that had been hewn out of the rock. Then he rolled a stone against the entrance to the tomb. Mary Magdalene and Mary the mother of Joses watched where he was laid.

Year C:
Luke 22:14-23:56 (short version Luke 23:1-49)

When the hour came, Jesus took his place at table with the apostles. He said to them, "I have eagerly desired to eat this Passover with you before I suffer, for, I tell you, I shall not eat it again until there is fulfillment in the kingdom of God." Then he took a cup, gave thanks, and said, "Take this and share it among yourselves; for I tell you that from this time on I shall not drink of the fruit of the vine until the kingdom of God comes." Then he took the bread, said the blessing, broke it, and gave it to them, saying, "This is my body, which will be given for you; do this in memory of me." And likewise the cup after they had eaten, saying, "This cup is the new covenant in my blood, which will be shed for you.

"And yet behold, the hand of the one who is to betray me is with me on the table; for the Son of Man indeed goes as it has been determined; but woe to that man by whom he is betrayed." And they began to debate among themselves who among them would do such a deed.

Then an argument broke out among them about which of them should be regarded as the greatest. He said to them, "The kings of the Gentiles lord it over them and those in authority over them are addressed as 'Benefactors'; but among you it shall not be so. Rather, let the greatest among you be as the youngest, and the leader as the servant. For who is greater: the one seated at table or the one who serves? Is it not the one seated at table? I am among you as the one who serves. It is you who have stood by me in my trials; and I confer a kingdom on you, just as my Father has conferred one on me, that you may eat and drink at my table in my kingdom; and you will sit on thrones judging the twelve tribes of Israel.

"Simon, Simon, behold Satan has demanded to sift all of you like wheat, but I have prayed that your own faith may not fail; and once you have turned back, you must strengthen your brothers." He said to him, "Lord, I am prepared to go to prison and to die with you." But he replied, "I tell you, Peter, before the cock crows this day, you will deny three times that you know me."

He said to them, "When I sent you forth without a money bag or a sack or sandals, were you in need of anything?" "No, nothing, " they replied. He said to them, "But now one who has a money bag should take it, and likewise a sack, and one who does not have a sword should sell his cloak and buy one. For I tell you that this Scripture must be fulfilled in me, namely, He was counted among the wicked; *and indeed what is written about me is coming to fulfillment." Then they said, "Lord, look, there are two swords here." But he replied, "It is enough!"*

Then going out, he went, as was his custom, to the Mount of Olives, and the disciples followed him. When he arrived at the place he said to them, "Pray that you may not undergo the test." After withdrawing about a stone's throw from them and kneeling, he prayed, saying, "Father, if you are willing, take this cup away from me; still, not my will but yours be done." And to strengthen him an angel from heaven appeared to him. He was in such agony and he prayed so fervently that his sweat became like drops of blood falling on the ground. When he rose from prayer and returned to his disciples, he found them sleeping from grief. He said to them, "Why are you sleeping? Get up and pray that you may not undergo the test."

While he was still speaking, a crowd approached and in front was one of the Twelve, a man named Judas. He went up to Jesus to kiss him. Jesus said to him, "Judas, are you betraying the Son of Man with a kiss?" His disciples realized what was about to happen, and they asked, "Lord, shall we strike with a sword?" And one of them struck the high priest's servant and cut off his right ear. But Jesus said in reply, "Stop, no more of this!" Then he touched the servant's ear and healed him. And Jesus said to the chief priests and temple guards and elders who had come for him, "Have you come out as against a robber, with swords and clubs? Day after day I was with you in the temple area, and you did not seize me, but this is your hour, the time for the power of darkness."

After arresting him they led him away and took him into the house of the high priest; Peter was following at a distance. They lit a fire in the middle of the courtyard and sat around it, and Peter sat down with them. When a maid saw him seated in the light, she looked intently at him and said, "This man too was with him." But he denied it saying,

"Woman, I do not know him." A short while later someone else saw him and said, "You too are one of them"; but Peter answered, "My friend, I am not." About an hour later, still another insisted, "Assuredly, this man too was with him, for he also is a Galilean." But Peter said, "My friend, I do not know what you are talking about." Just as he was saying this, the cock crowed, and the Lord turned and looked at Peter; and Peter remembered the word of the Lord, how he had said to him, "Before the cock crows today, you will deny me three times." He went out and began to weep bitterly. The men who held Jesus in custody were ridiculing and beating him. They blindfolded him and questioned him, saying, "Prophesy! Who is it that struck you?" And they reviled him in saying many other things against him.

When day came the council of elders of the people met, both chief priests and scribes, and they brought him before their Sanhedrin. They said, "If you are the Christ, tell us, " but he replied to them, "If I tell you, you will not believe, and if I question, you will not respond. But from this time on the Son of Man will be seated at the right hand of the power of God." They all asked, "Are you then the Son of God?" He replied to them, "You say that I am." Then they said, "What further need have we for testimony? We have heard it from his own mouth."

Then the whole assembly of them arose and brought him before Pilate. They brought charges against him, saying, "We found this man misleading our people; he opposes the payment of taxes to Caesar and maintains that he is the Christ, a king." Pilate asked him, "Are you the king of the Jews?" He said to him in reply, "You say so." Pilate then addressed the chief priests and the crowds, "I find this man not guilty." But they were adamant and said, "He is inciting the people with his teaching throughout all Judea, from Galilee where he began even to here."

On hearing this Pilate asked if the man was a Galilean; and upon learning that he was under Herod's jurisdiction, he sent him to Herod who was in Jerusalem at that time. Herod was very glad to see Jesus; he had been wanting to see him for a long time, for he had heard about him and had been hoping to see him perform some sign. He questioned him at length, but he gave him no answer. The chief priests *and scribes, meanwhile, stood by accusing him harshly. Herod and his soldiers treated him contemptuously and mocked him, and after clothing him in resplendent garb, he sent him back to Pilate. Herod and Pilate became friends that very day, even though they had been enemies formerly. Pilate then summoned the chief priests, the rulers, and the people and said to them, "You brought this man to me and accused him of inciting the people to revolt. I have conducted my investigation in your presence and have not found this man guilty of the charges you have brought against him, nor did Herod, for he sent him back to us. So no capital crime has been committed by him. Therefore I shall have him flogged and then release him."*

But all together they shouted out, "Away with this man! Release Barabbas to us." — Now Barabbas had been imprisoned for a rebellion that had taken place in the city and for murder. — Again Pilate addressed them, still wishing to release Jesus, but they continued their shouting, "Crucify him! Crucify him!" Pilate addressed them a third time, "What evil has this man done? I found him guilty of no capital crime. Therefore I shall have him flogged and then release him." With loud shouts, however, they persisted in calling for his crucifixion, and their voices prevailed. The verdict of Pilate was that their demand should be granted. So he released the man who had been imprisoned for rebellion and murder, for whom they asked, and he handed Jesus over to them to deal with as they wished.

As they led him away they took hold of a certain Simon, a Cyrenian, who was coming in from the country; and after laying the cross on him, they made him carry it behind Jesus. A large crowd of people followed Jesus, including many women who mourned and lamented him. Jesus turned to them and said, "Daughters of Jerusalem, do not weep for me; weep instead for yourselves and for your children for indeed, the days are coming when people will say, 'Blessed are the barren, the wombs that never bore and the breasts that never nursed.' At that time people will say to the mountains, 'Fall upon us!' and to the hills, 'Cover us!' for if these things are done when the wood is green what will happen when it is dry?" Now two others, both criminals, were led away with him to be executed.

When they came to the place called the Skull, they crucified him and the criminals there, one on his right, the other on his left. Then Jesus said, "Father, forgive them, they know not what they do." They divided his garments by casting lots. The people stood by and watched; the rulers, meanwhile, sneered at him and said, "He saved others, let him save himself if he is the chosen one, the Christ of God." Even the soldiers jeered at him. As they approached to offer him wine they called out, "If you are King of the Jews, save yourself." Above him there was an inscription that read, "This is the King of the Jews."

Now one of the criminals hanging there reviled Jesus, saying, "Are you not the Christ? Save yourself and us." The other, however, rebuking him, said in reply, "Have you no fear of God, for you are subject to the same condemnation? And indeed, we have been condemned justly, for the sentence we received corresponds to our crimes, but this man has done nothing criminal." Then he said, "Jesus, remember me when you come into your kingdom." He replied to him, "Amen, I say to you, today you will be with me in Paradise."

It was now about noon and darkness came over the whole land until three in the afternoon because of an eclipse of the sun. Then the veil of the temple was torn down the middle. Jesus cried out in a loud voice, "Father, into your hands I commend my spirit"; and when he had said this he breathed his last.

(Here all kneel and pause for a short time)

The centurion who witnessed what had happened glorified God and said, "This man was innocent beyond doubt." When all the people who had gathered for this spectacle saw what had happened, they returned home beating their breasts; but all his acquaintances stood at a distance, including the women who had followed him from Galilee and saw these events.

Now there was a virtuous and righteous man named Joseph who, though he was a member of the council, had not consented to their plan of action. He came from the Jewish town of Arimathea and was awaiting the kingdom of God. He went to Pilate and asked for the body of Jesus. After he had taken the body down, he wrapped it in a linen cloth and laid him in a rock-hewn tomb in which no one had yet been buried. It was the day of preparation, and the sabbath was about to begin. The women who had come from Galilee with him followed behind, and when they had seen the tomb and the way in which his body was laid in it, they returned and prepared spices and perfumed oils. Then they rested on the sabbath according to the commandment.

Holy Saturday Readings

Alternate Psalm after the first reading of Genesis 1:1-2:2:
Psalm 33: 4-5, 6-7, 12-13, 20 and 22

R. (5b) The earth is full of the goodness of the Lord.

Upright is the word of the LORD,
    and all his works are trustworthy.
He loves justice and right;
    of the kindness of the LORD the earth is full.

R. The earth is full of the goodness of the Lord.

By the word of the LORD the heavens were made;
    by the breath of his mouth all their host.
He gathers the waters of the sea as in a flask;
    in cellars he confines the deep.

R. The earth is full of the goodness of the Lord.

Blessed the nation whose God is the LORD,
    the people he has chosen for his own inheritance.
From heaven the LORD looks down;
    he sees all mankind.

R. The earth is full of the goodness of the Lord.

Our soul waits for the LORD,
    who is our help and our shield.

May your kindness, O LORD, be upon us
   who have put our hope in you.

R. The earth is full of the goodness of the Lord.

Alternate Psalm after the seventh reading of Ezekiel 36:16-17A, 18-28:
(if there are no baptisms)
Isaiah 12:2-3, 4BCD, 5-6

R. (3) You will draw water joyfully from the springs of salvation.

God indeed is my savior;
   I am confident and unafraid.
My strength and my courage is the LORD,
   and he has been my savior.
With joy you will draw water
   at the fountain of salvation.

R. You will draw water joyfully from the springs of salvation.

Give thanks to the LORD, acclaim his name;
   among the nations make known his deeds,
   proclaim how exalted is his name.

R. You will draw water joyfully from the springs of salvation.

Sing praise to the LORD for his glorious achievement;
   let this be known throughout all the earth.
Shout with exultation, O city of Zion,
   for great in your midst
   is the Holy One of Israel!

R. You will draw water joyfully from the springs of salvation.

or Psalm 51:12-13, 14-15, 18-19

R. (12a) Create a clean heart in me, O God.

A clean heart create for me, O God,
   and a steadfast spirit renew within me.

Cast me not out from your presence,
*   and your Holy Spirit take not from me.*

R. Create a clean heart in me, O God.

Give me back the joy of your salvation,
*   and a willing spirit sustain in me.*
I will teach transgressors your ways,
*   and sinners shall return to you.*

R. Create a clean heart in me, O God.

For you are not pleased with sacrifices;
*   should I offer a holocaust, you would not accept it.*
My sacrifice, O God, is a contrite spirit;
*   a heart contrite and humbled, O God, you will not spurn.*

R. Create a clean heart in me, O God.

Holy Saturday Gospel:

Year B:
- *Mark 16:1-7*

> *When the sabbath was over, Mary Magdalene, Mary, the mother of James, and Salome bought spices so that they might go and anoint him. Very early when the sun had risen, on the first day of the week, they came to the tomb. They were saying to one another, "Who will roll back the stone for us from the entrance to the tomb?" When they looked up, they saw that the stone had been rolled back; it was very large. On entering the tomb they saw a young man sitting on the right side, clothed in a white robe, and they were utterly amazed. He said to them, "Do not be amazed! You seek Jesus of Nazareth, the crucified. He has been raised; he is not here. Behold, the place where they laid him. But go and tell his disciples and Peter, 'He is going before you to Galilee; there you will see him, as he told you.'"*

Year C:
- *Luke 24:1-12*

> At daybreak on the first day of the week the women took the spices they had prepared and went to the tomb. They found the stone rolled away from the tomb; but when they entered, they did not find the body of the Lord Jesus. While they were puzzling over this, behold, two men in dazzling garments appeared to them. They were terrified and bowed their faces to the ground. They said to them, "Why do you seek the living one among the dead? He is not here, but he has been raised. Remember what he said to you while he was still in Galilee, that the Son of Man must be handed over to sinners and be crucified, and rise on the third day." And they remembered his words. Then they returned from the tomb and announced all these things to the eleven and to all the others. The women were Mary Magdalene, Joanna, and Mary the mother of James; the other who accompanied them also told this to the apostles, but their story seemed like nonsense and they did not believe them. But Peter got up and ran to the tomb, bent down, and saw the burial cloths alone; then he went home amazed at what had happened.

Easter Sunday Readings

New Testament alternate reading:
- *1 Cor 5: 6B-8*

> Brothers and sisters: Do you not know that a little yeast leavens all the dough? Clear out the old yeast, so that you may become a fresh batch of dough, inasmuch as you are unleavened. For our paschal lamb, Christ, has been sacrificed. Therefore, let us celebrate the feast, not with the old yeast, the yeast of malice and wickedness, but with the unleavened bread of sincerity and truth.

Gospel: Alternate readings: Year A: Matthew 28:1-10; Year B: Mark 16:1-7; Year C: Luke 24:1-12; All years: Luke 24:13-35

■ Matthew 28:1-10

After the sabbath, as the first day of the week was dawning, Mary Magdalene and the other Mary came to see the tomb. And behold, there was a great earthquake; for an angel of the Lord descended from heaven, approached, rolled back the stone, and sat upon it. His appearance was like lightning and his clothing was white as snow. The guards were shaken with fear of him and became like dead men. Then the angel said to the women in reply, "Do not be afraid! I know that you are seeking Jesus the crucified. He is not here, for he has been raised just as he said. Come and see the place where he lay. Then go quickly and tell his disciples, 'He has been raised from the dead, and he is going before you to Galilee; there you will see him.' Behold, I have told you." Then they went away quickly from the tomb, fearful yet overjoyed, and ran to announce this to his disciples. And behold, Jesus met them on their way and greeted them. They approached, embraced his feet, and did him homage. Then Jesus said to them, "Do not be afraid. Go tell my brothers to go to Galilee, and there they will see me."

■ Mark 16:1-7

When the sabbath was over, Mary Magdalene, Mary, the mother of James, and Salome bought spices so that they might go and anoint him. Very early when the sun had risen, on the first day of the week, they came to the tomb. They were saying to one another, "Who will roll back the stone for us from the entrance to the tomb?" When they looked up, they saw that the stone had been rolled back; it was very large. On entering the tomb they saw a young man sitting on the right side, clothed in a white robe, and they were utterly amazed. He said to them, "Do not be amazed! You seek Jesus of Nazareth, the crucified. He has been raised; he is not here. Behold the place where they laid him. But go and tell his disciples and Peter, 'He is going before you to Galilee; there you will see him, as he told you.'"

- *Luke 24:1-12*

    But at daybreak on the first day of the week they took the spices they had prepared and went to the tomb. They found the stone rolled away from the tomb; but when they entered, they did not find the body of the Lord Jesus. While they were puzzling over this, behold, two men in dazzling garments appeared to them. They were terrified and bowed their faces to the ground. They said to them, "Why do you seek the living one among the dead? He is not here, but he has been raised. Remember what he said to you while he was still in Galilee, that the Son of Man must be handed over to sinners and be crucified, and rise on the third day." And they remembered his words. Then they returned from the tomb and announced all these things to the eleven and to all the others. The women were Mary Magdalene, Joanna, and Mary the mother of James; the others who accompanied them also told this to the apostles, but their story seemed like nonsense and they did not believe them. But Peter got up and ran to the tomb, bent down, and saw the burial cloths alone; then he went home amazed at what had happened.

- *Luke 24:13-35*

    That very day, the first day of the week, two of Jesus' disciples were going to a village seven miles from Jerusalem called Emmaus, and they were conversing about all the things that had occurred. And it happened that while they were conversing and debating, Jesus himself drew near and walked with them, but their eyes were prevented from recognizing him. He asked them, "What are you discussing as you walk along?" They stopped, looking downcast. One of them, named Cleopas, said to him in reply, "Are you the only visitor to Jerusalem who does not know of the things that have taken place there in these days?" And he replied to them, "What sort of things?" They said to him, "The things that happened to Jesus the Nazarene, who was a prophet mighty in deed and word before God and all the people, how our chief priests and rulers both handed him over to a sentence of death and crucified him. But we were hoping that he would be the one to redeem Israel; and besides all this, it is now the third day since this took place. Some women from our group, however, have astounded us: they were *at the tomb early in the morning and did not find his body; they came back and reported that they had indeed seen a vision of angels who announced that he was alive. Then some of those with us went to the tomb and found things just as the women had described, but him they did not see." And he said to them, "Oh, how foolish you are! How slow of heart to believe all that the prophets spoke! Was it not necessary that the Christ should suffer these things and enter into his glory?" Then beginning with Moses and all the prophets, he interpreted to them what referred to him in all the Scriptures. As they approached the village to which they were going, he gave the impression that he was going on farther. But they urged him, "Stay with us, for it is nearly evening and the day is almost over." So he went in to stay with them. And it happened that, while he was with them at table, he took bread, said the blessing, broke it, and gave it to them. With that their eyes were opened and they recognized him, but he vanished from their sight. Then they said to each other, "Were not our hearts burning within us while he spoke to us on the way and opened the Scriptures to us?" So they set out at once and returned to Jerusalem where they found gathered together the eleven and those with them who were saying, "The Lord has truly been raised and has appeared to Simon!" Then the two recounted what had taken place on the way and how he was made known to them in the breaking of bread.*

APPENDIX B

Scripture References

Biblical References

Isaiah 62:11 –
The LORD has proclaimed
    to the ends of the earth:
Say to daughter Zion,
    "See, your savior comes!
See, his reward is with him,
    his recompense before him."

Zechariah 9:9-13 –
Exult greatly, O daughter Zion!
    Shout for joy, O daughter Jerusalem!
Behold: your king is coming to you,
    a just savior is he,
Humble, and riding on a donkey,
    on a colt, the foal of a donkey.
He shall banish the chariot from Ephraim,
    and the horse from Jerusalem;
The warrior's bow will be banished,
    and he will proclaim peace to the nations.
His dominion will be from sea to sea,
    and from the River to the ends of the earth.

As for you, by the blood of your covenant,
    I have freed your prisoners from a waterless pit.
Return to a fortress,
    O prisoners of hope;
This very day, I announce
    I am restoring double to you.
For I have bent Judah as my bow,
    I have set Ephraim as its arrow;
I will arouse your sons, O Zion,
    against your sons, O Yavan,
and I will use you as a warrior's sword.

Zechariah 12:10-13:1

I will pour out on the house of David and on the inhabitants of Jerusalem a spirit of mercy and supplication, so that when they look on him whom they have thrust through, they will mourn for him as one mourns for an only child, and they will grieve for him as one grieves over a firstborn.

On that day the mourning in Jerusalem will be as great as the mourning for Hadadrimmon in the plain of Megiddo. And the land shall mourn, each family apart: the family of the house of David, and their women; the family of the house of Nathan, and their women; the family of the house of Levi, and their women; the family of Shimei, and their women; and all the rest of the families, each family apart, and the women apart.

On that day a fountain will be opened for the house of David and the inhabitants of Jerusalem, to purify from sin and uncleanness.

Psalm 22

For the leader; according to "The deer of the dawn."* A psalm of David.

My God, my God, why have you abandoned me?
  Why so far from my call for help,
  from my cries of anguish?
My God, I call by day, but you do not answer;
  by night, but I have no relief.
Yet you are enthroned as the Holy One;
  you are the glory of Israel.
In you our fathers trusted;
  they trusted and you rescued them.
To you they cried out and they escaped;
  in you they trusted and were not disappointed.
But I am a worm, not a man,
  scorned by men, despised by the people.
All who see me mock me;
  they curl their lips and jeer;

they shake their heads at me:
"He relied on the LORD—let him deliver him;
if he loves him, let him rescue him."
For you drew me forth from the womb,
made me safe at my mother's breasts.
Upon you I was thrust from the womb;
since my mother bore me you are my God.
Do not stay far from me,
for trouble is near,
and there is no one to help.

II

Many bulls surround me;
fierce bulls of Bashan encircle me.
They open their mouths against me,
lions that rend and roar.
Like water my life drains away;
all my bones are disjointed.
My heart has become like wax,
it melts away within me.
As dry as a potsherd is my throat;
my tongue cleaves to my palate;
you lay me in the dust of death.
Dogs surround me;
a pack of evildoers closes in on me.
They have pierced my hands and my feet
I can count all my bones.
They stare at me and gloat;
they divide my garments among them;
for my clothing they cast lots.
But you, LORD, do not stay far off;
my strength, come quickly to help me.
Deliver my soul from the sword,
my life from the grip of the dog.
Save me from the lion's mouth,
my poor life from the horns of wild bulls.

III
Then I will proclaim your name to my brethren;
  in the assembly I will praise you:
"You who fear the LORD, give praise!
  All descendants of Jacob, give honor;
  show reverence, all descendants of Israel!
For he has not spurned or disdained
  the misery of this poor wretch,
Did not turn away from me,
  but heard me when I cried out.
I will offer praise in the great assembly;
  my vows I will fulfill before those who fear him.
The poor will eat their fill;
  those who seek the LORD will offer praise.
  May your hearts enjoy life forever!"

IV

All the ends of the earth
  will remember and turn to the LORD;
All the families of nations
  will bow low before him.
For kingship belongs to the LORD,
  the ruler over the nations.
All who sleep in the earth
  will bow low before God;
All who have gone down into the dust
  will kneel in homage.
And I will live for the LORD;
  my descendants will serve you.
The generation to come will be told of the Lord,
  that they may proclaim to a people yet unborn
  the deliverance you have brought.

John 6:66-68
As a result of this, many [of] his disciples returned to their former way of life and no longer accompanied him. Jesus then said to the Twelve, "Do you also want to leave?" Simon Peter answered him, "Master, to whom shall we go? You have the words of eternal life."

APPENDIX C

Contradictions in the Passion of Jesus

1. Judas comes with an army of soldiers, and Jesus is in control of the confrontation – "Whom are you looking for?"
2. Jesus identifies himself, and the soldiers fall to the ground.
3. Jesus commands the soldiers to let the others go, and the soldiers obey.
4. The soldiers tie Jesus up, even though He gave no resistance.
5. Caiaphas was high priest, yet the first person to judge Jesus was Caiaphas' father-in-law.
6. Caiaphas prophesied Jesus' role when he said, "One man should die rather than the people." This is exactly what was happening – not that the people would die because of the Roman soldiers, but that they would die because of their sin, and Jesus was about to take their place.
7. Peter denies that he is a disciple of Jesus three times, even though he is one of Jesus' inner circle.
8. Jesus spoke in public, during the day, in the temple. The high priest questions and accuses him in private, in the middle of the night, in his home.
9. Jesus speaks truth and is struck for it.
10. The Jews accusing Jesus do not enter the praetorium. Entering will defile them, so they remain outside in order to remain clean to celebrate the Passover. Yet they are demanding the life of an innocent man on false charges, and they can't see the defilement of that action.
11. When Pilate asks what the charges are, the priests answer, "If he were not a criminal, we would not have handed him over to you." No parent would accept this kind of a non-answer.
12. Pilate asks Jesus what He did: "Your own nation and the chief priests handed you over to me. What have you done?" He's getting the accusation from the accused, not the accusers.

13. Pilate finds no guilt in Jesus, but he doesn't release Him.
14. The Jews demand the release of Barabbas. His name means "Son of the father." The Son of the Father is the innocent one. They are just slightly off the mark.
15. The soldiers cry, "Hail, King of the Jews!" Pilate says on many occasions, "I find no guilt in him." The only ones proclaiming the truth about Jesus are the non-Jewish people in the story.
16. Pilate tries to release Jesus, but the chief priests won't let him. Then he goes to Jesus and says, "Do you not know that I have the power to release you, and I have power to crucify you?" It doesn't look like he has much power, does it?
17. Pilate places Jesus on the judge's bench, not in front of the judge's bench. Again, the true judge is Jesus — not Pilate, not the chief priests. The judgment is about to be handed down and received by the same person.
18. "Behold, your King!"
19. The chief priests say, "We have no king but Caesar." Their God has been replaced.
20. The inscription proclaims the true nature of Jesus – "King of the Jews." This is the only time in the story that Pilate asserts his authority, and it is allowed to stand.
21. The wine given to Jesus is on a hyssop branch. Hyssop was used to spread the blood of the lamb on the doorposts for the Passover. Jesus' blood had been spilled and offered, and He gave His life over as He received the wine.

APPENDIX
D

Parallels to Jesus in the Story of the Sacrifice of Isaac

1. Abraham is asked to offer his only son, whom he loves, as a sacrifice. God's only beloved Son is offered as a sacrifice.
2. Abraham travels for three days. Jesus is dead for three days.
3. The sacrifice of Isaac will be made on a hill. Jesus is crucified on a hill.
4. Moriah is believed to be the location of Jerusalem.
5. Abraham takes a donkey, his son, and the wood for the sacrifice. Jesus arrives in Jerusalem on a donkey.
6. Isaac carries the wood for his own sacrifice on his shoulders. Jesus carries His own cross on His shoulders.
7. Isaac is placed on the wood for the sacrifice. Jesus is placed on the wood of the cross.
8. "God will provide the sheep for the holocaust." Jesus is the Lamb of God, provided by God.
9. The ram is caught by its horns in a thicket, with its head surrounded by thorns. A crown of thorns encircles Jesus' head.
10. Abraham's devotion was made clear because he was willing to offer his only beloved son. God shows us His love by offering His only beloved Son.
11. God halted the sacrifice of Isaac. We did not stop the sacrifice of Jesus. We demanded that it be completed.

Notes for Holy Week

As you go through each lesson, come here and write down the things that touched you the most. Write down the things you want to look for as you attend the Mass. Bring them with you during Holy Week and watch the story unfold.

Palm Sunday

Holy Thursday

Good Friday

Holy Saturday

Easter Sunday